JAMESTOWN

*H*eritage

READERS

Book C

Lee Mountain, Ed.D.
University of Houston, Texas

Sharon Crawley, Ed.D.
Florida Atlantic University

Edward Fry, Ph.D.
Professor Emeritus
Rutgers University

Jamestown Publishers
Providence, Rhode Island

Favorite Children's Classics

ILLUSTRATED BY THE BEST ARTISTS
FROM THE PAST AND PRESENT

Jamestown Heritage Readers, Book C
Catalog No. 953
Catalog No. 953H, Hardcover Edition

Cover and text design by Deborah Hulsey Christie
Cover and border illustrations by Pamela R. Levy

Printed in the United States of America

2   3   4   5   6   HA   96   95   94   93   92

ISBN 0-89061-953-0
ISBN 0-89061-712-0, Hardcover Edition

C·O·N·T·E·N·T·S

ONE
Tales Retold

TWO

Here and There, Then and Now

THREE
The Whole Chapter

FOUR
Numbers, Nature, and Nonsense

UNIT ONE
Tales Retold

The Emperor's New Clothes

by

HANS CHRISTIAN ANDERSEN

Once upon a time there was an emperor who loved new clothes. He had a different coat for each day of the year. He had so many pairs of shoes that they covered the floor of a large room, and still he kept buying new clothes.

He cared more about clothes than about anything else.

One day two men came to the city where the emperor lived.

The two men had heard many stories about the emperor, and they had thought of a way to trick him into paying them lots of money.

The men told the emperor's guard that they were weavers.

"We can weave cloth more beautiful than you have ever seen before," said one of the men. "The emperor has nothing as fine as the clothes we could make for him. But the cloth we weave is not only beautiful. It is also magical."

"Oh, my!" said the guard. "Think of that! How does the magic work?"

"Only people who are wise and good can see our cloth," said the first weaver. "People who are foolish and bad cannot see it."

"The emperor must hear about this," said the guard. He took them into the castle.

The emperor heard their story.

Then he said, "You must weave this cloth for me at once. It will be beautiful, and I will like wearing the fine new clothes made from your cloth. But it will also help me know which of my people are foolish and bad."

He gave them money to begin their work.

They set up looms. They acted as if they were weaving, but they were really just making noise.

The emperor heard the noise. "I should like to know what this cloth looks like," thought the emperor. "I will send my guard to find out. I am certain that he is a good and wise man, so he will be able to see the cloth."

The guard went into the room where the two men sat working. "Dear me!" thought he, opening his eyes wide. "Their looms look empty. I can see no cloth." But he did not say what he was thinking.

One of the men said, "Step closer. Did you ever see more beautiful colors?"

The poor guard rubbed his eyes, but he could see nothing, for there was nothing there.

13

"Dear, dear!" he said to himself. "Am I foolish? Or can it be that I am bad? I have never thought so. And no one must know it. I surely must not let the emperor know. I must not say that I cannot see the cloth!"

"Have you nothing to say about our cloth?" asked one of the men.

"Oh, it is beautiful!" said the guard. "Most beautiful! I will tell the emperor what fine work you are doing."

"We are happy to hear that," said the weavers. Then they talked on and on about the colors in the cloth.

The guard listened well so that he could tell it all to the emperor, and the emperor was pleased when he heard.

The men now wanted more money. They said they needed it for gold and silver to use in their weaving, but they really put it in their pockets. Then they went on as they had before, working at the empty looms.

Many of the emperor's men peeked in to
see the cloth. It was the same with them as
with the guard. They looked and looked. But
because there was nothing on the looms to
see, they could see nothing.

But none of them wanted to seem foolish or
bad. So each went back to the emperor, saying
how beautiful the cloth was. Soon everyone in
the city was talking about the beautiful cloth.

15

The emperor decided that he wanted to see it for himself while it was still on the looms. With all his followers, he walked into the room where the men were weaving.

"Is it not beautiful!" said the guard, who had been there first. "What colors!" And he pointed to the empty looms, for he thought everyone else could see the cloth quite well.

"What!" thought the emperor to himself. "I can see nothing. Am I foolish and bad? If so, it is not right for me to be emperor. I must not let my followers know. I must make-believe."

He nodded and smiled. "Fine work," he said to the weavers. "Very beautiful!" He would not say that he could see nothing.

All his followers shook their heads too. "Most beautiful cloth" went from mouth to mouth. They said that new clothes should soon be made from it, and the emperor should wear the new clothes in a great parade.

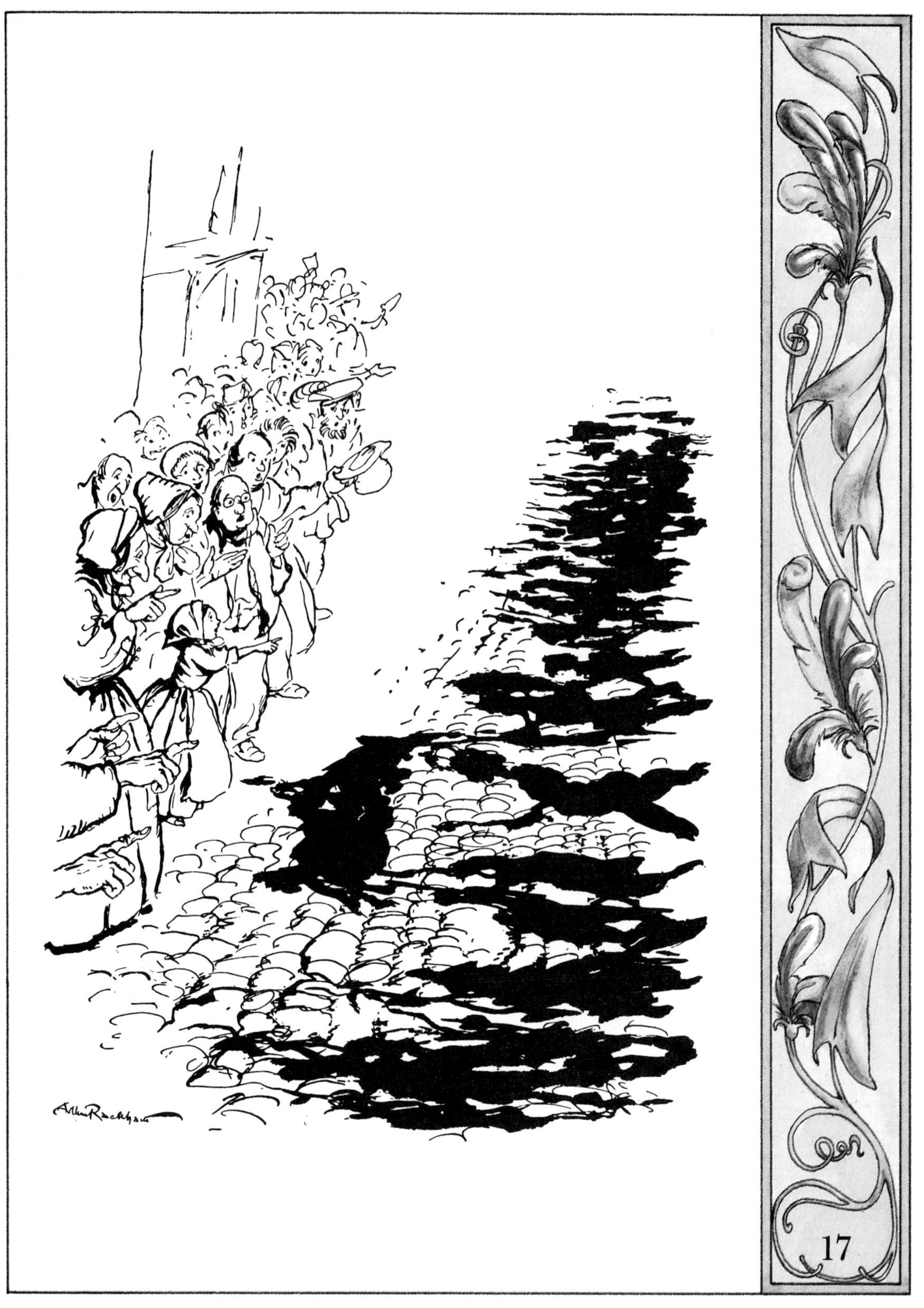
Arthur Rackham

He should walk through the center of the city. Then everyone could see his new clothes.

The night before the parade, the weavers made believe they were finishing the emperor's new clothes. They seemed to be hurrying as fast as they could.

At last they said, "The clothes are ready. We will take them to the emperor."

The emperor was waiting to put on his clothes. "You may help me get dressed," he said to the weavers.

"See how well the clothes fit," said one of the men.

"Oh, yes," said the guard.

"A beautiful fit," said the emperor's followers. They would not have anyone know that they could see nothing.

"Who will carry the emperor's train?" asked one of the weavers. "This cloth is too fine to touch the ground."

Two guards hurried to help. They put
their hands near the ground as if they were
picking up the train. Then they acted as if
they were holding a long train of cloth.

People had come from far and near
to see this parade. Everyone was talking
of the emperor's new clothes. No one
wished to have it noted that he could see
no clothes.

"But he has nothing on," said a little child at last.

"Hush, child," said the father. But the people started telling one another what the child had said.

"But he has nothing on," the people cried out at last.

The emperor heard. He knew that they were right. But he did not know how he could turn back now, so he went on with the parade. And his guards kept walking behind him, holding up the train that was not there at all.

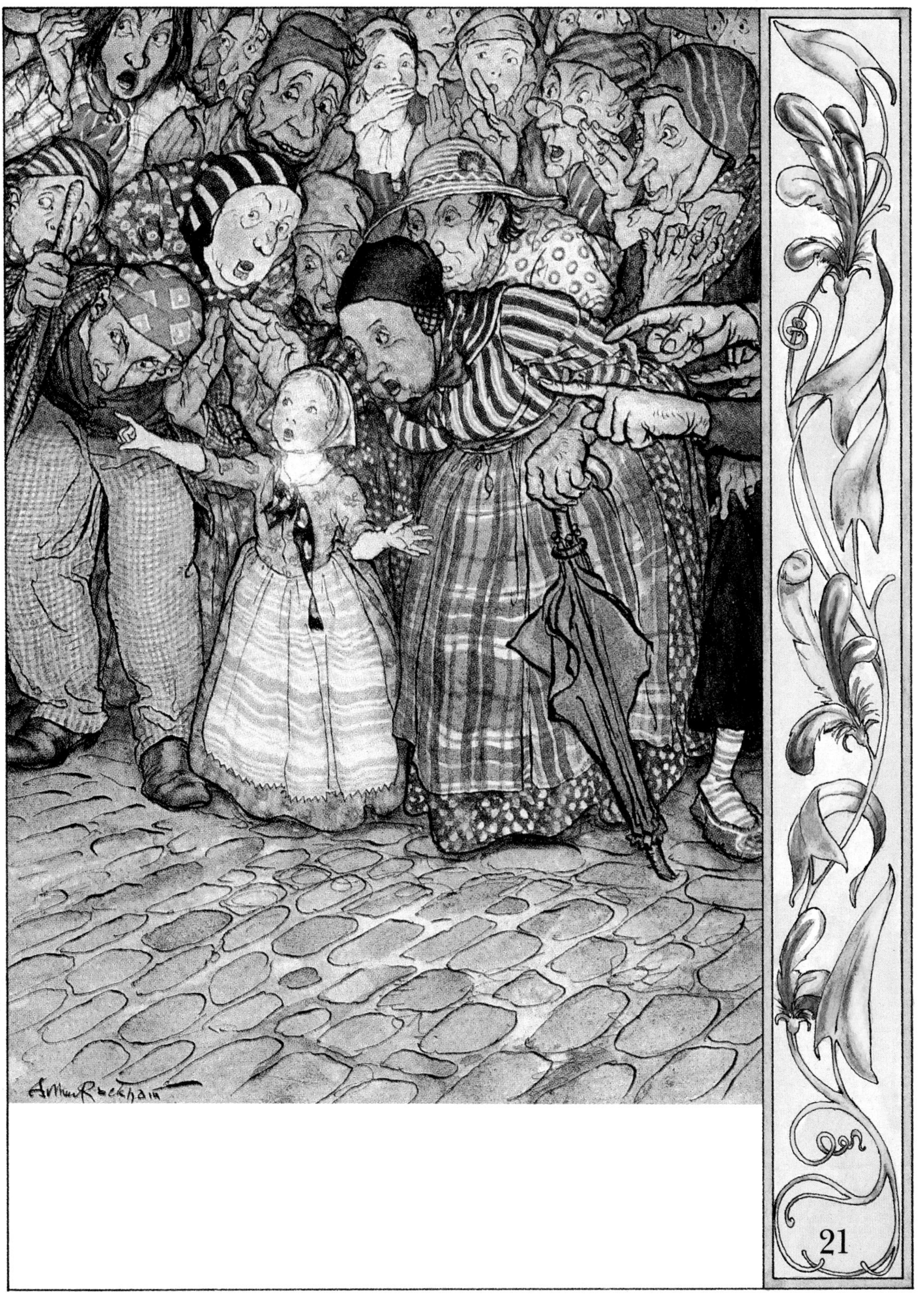
Arthur Rackham

Father William

from

ALICE'S ADVENTURES IN WONDERLAND

by

LEWIS CARROLL

"**Y**ou are old, father William,"
   the young man said.
"And your hair has become very white.
   And yet you insist you can
      stand on your head.
   Do you think, at your age, it is right?"

"In my youth," father William
replied to his son,
"I feared it might injure my brain.
But now that I'm perfectly
sure I have none,
Why, I do it again and again."

The Cat That Walked by Himself

by

RUDYARD KIPLING

Long ago all the animals were wild. The Dog was wild, and the Horse was wild. The Cow was wild, and the Pig was wild—as wild as wild could be.

But the wildest of all the wild animals was the Cat. He walked by himself, and all places were alike to him.

One night, out in the Wet Wild Woods, all the wild animals met. They could see the light of a fire in a cave near the river, and they could see a Man and a Woman by the fire.

Wild Dog smelled the smell of meat on the fire. "I think I will go have a look," he said. "What I smell is good. Cat, come with me."

"No!" said the Cat. "I am the Cat who walks by himself, and all places are alike to me."

"Then we can never be friends again," said Wild Dog, and he ran off to the cave.

The Cat thought, "All places are alike to me. Why should I not go too? I can see and look and come away at my liking." So he went after Wild Dog very softly, and he hid himself where he could hear what was said.

Wild Dog reached the cave. He smelled the beautiful smell of cooked meat.

The Woman asked Wild Dog, "Wild Thing out of the Wild Woods, what do you want?"

Wild Dog said, "Oh, my Enemy and Wife of my Enemy, what is this that smells so good?"

The Woman threw a bone to Wild Dog. "This is what smells so good," she said.

Wild Dog chewed on the bone. It was very good indeed. "Oh, my Enemy and Wife of my Enemy," he said. "Please give me more."

The Woman said, "Will you help my Man hunt? Will you guard this cave?"

"Ah," thought the Cat. "This is a very wise Woman, but she is not so wise as I am."

Wild Dog said, "I will help you hunt, and I will guard your cave."

"Ah," thought the Cat. "That is a very foolish Dog." Then Cat went back through the Wet Wild Woods, walking by himself.

When the Man woke up, he said, "What is Wild Dog doing here?"

The Woman said, "His name is now First Friend. He will help you hunt."

The next day the Woman cut green grass and dried it by the fire. Then she sat at the mouth of the cave and made a harness out of hides. And she waited.

Now, out in the Wild Woods Wild Horse said, "I will go see why Wild Dog has not returned. Cat, come with me."

"No!" said the Cat. "I am the Cat who walks by himself, and all places are alike to me." But he followed Wild Horse very softly, and he hid himself where he could hear what was said.

When the Woman heard Wild Horse coming, she smiled. "Wild Thing out of the Wild Woods, what do you want?" she asked.

Wild Horse said, "Where is Wild Dog?"

The Woman laughed. "You did not come here for Wild Dog, but for this good grass."

Wild Horse said, "That is true."

"Wear this harness," said the woman. "Carry my Man when he goes hunting."

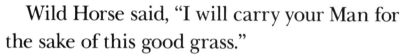

The woman held up the grass. "Then you can eat this each day."

"Ah," thought the Cat. "This is a clever Woman, but she is not so clever as I am."

Wild Horse said, "I will carry your Man for the sake of this good grass."

"Ah," thought the Cat. "That is a very foolish Horse." And Cat went back through the Wet Wild Woods, walking by himself.

Then the Man and the Dog came back from hunting. "What is Wild Horse doing here?" asked the Man.

"His name is now First Servant," said the Woman. "He will always carry us. Ride on his back when you go hunting."

The next day Wild Cow came to the cave, and the Cat followed and hid just as before.

Wild Cow said that she would give milk each day for the good grass, and the Cat walked away, as before.

Then the Man and the Horse and the Dog came home from hunting. They asked the same questions as before.

The Woman said, "Her name is now Giver of Good Food. She will always give us warm, white milk."

The next day Cat walked to the cave. He saw the Woman milking the Cow. He saw the man in the back of the cave. He saw the light of the fire, and he smelled the smell of warm, white milk.

The Cat said, "Where did my Wild Friends go?"

The Woman laughed. "Wild Thing out of the Wild Woods, go back to the Woods."

The Cat said, "I am the Cat who walks by himself, and I wish to come into your cave."

The Woman laughed. "You are the Cat who walks by himself. All places are alike to you. You are not a Friend or a Servant. Go away and walk by yourself."

Then the Cat pretended to be sorry. "Must I never come into the cave?" he said. "Must I never sit by the fire and drink warm milk? You are wise. You should be kind, too."

The Woman said, "If ever I say one word in your praise, you may come into the cave."

"And if you say two words in my praise?" asked the Cat.

"I never shall," said the Woman. "But if I do, you may sit by the fire in the cave."

"And if you say three words?" asked the Cat.

"I never shall," said the Woman. "But if I do, you may always drink the warm, white milk."

Then the Cat said, "Let the fire in this cave remember what the Wife of my Enemy has said." And he went away.

31

"I will do so," said the Woman, "but only because I must get my Baby to stop crying. I will not thank you for it."

She gave a ball of string to the Cat. He ran after it and patted it with his paws. Soon the Baby was laughing as loudly as he had been crying.

The Woman smiled. "That was well done. You are very clever, Cat."

That second the smoke of the fire came down with a puff. The fire remembered the bargain the Woman had made. When it cleared, there was the Cat, sitting by the fire.

Then the Woman was very, very angry. She would not even look at the Cat. She thought to herself that she would never, never say a third word in praise of the Cat.

The cave was very still. A little mouse came out and ran toward the sleeping Baby. He stopped just short of the Baby's hand.

"Should I let this little mouse chew on your Baby's thumb?" said the Cat.

"No! No, indeed," cried the Woman. "Kill it. Do not let that mouse get one bit closer to my Baby. Eat it now!"

The Cat made one jump. That was the end of the mouse.

"All my thanks to you, Cat!" said the Woman.

That second the fire puffed and popped. Now the Cat was drinking warm, white milk from the bowl by the fire.

That night, when the Man and the Dog came into the cave, the Woman told them of her bargain with the Cat.

"Wait a minute," said the Dog. "The Cat has not made a bargain with me." He showed his teeth. "You must keep on catching every mouse you see," he said to the Cat. "You must be good to the Baby or I will hunt you. And when I catch you, I will bite you."

The Cat looked at the Dog's teeth. They looked very long and sharp. He said, "I will catch every mouse I see, and I will be good to the Baby as long as he does not pull my tail. But still I am the Cat who walks by himself, and all places are alike to me."

"Not when I am near," said the Dog. "If you had not said that, I would have shut my mouth forever. But now I am going to hunt you up a tree whenever I meet you, and so shall all Dogs after me."

Then the Cat ran out of the cave, and the Dog chased him up a tree. And from that day to this, dogs will chase cats up trees.

And the Cat keeps his side of the bargain. He will catch each mouse that he sees, and he will be good to babies, as long as they do not pull his tail. But he is still the Cat that walks by himself, and all places are alike to him.

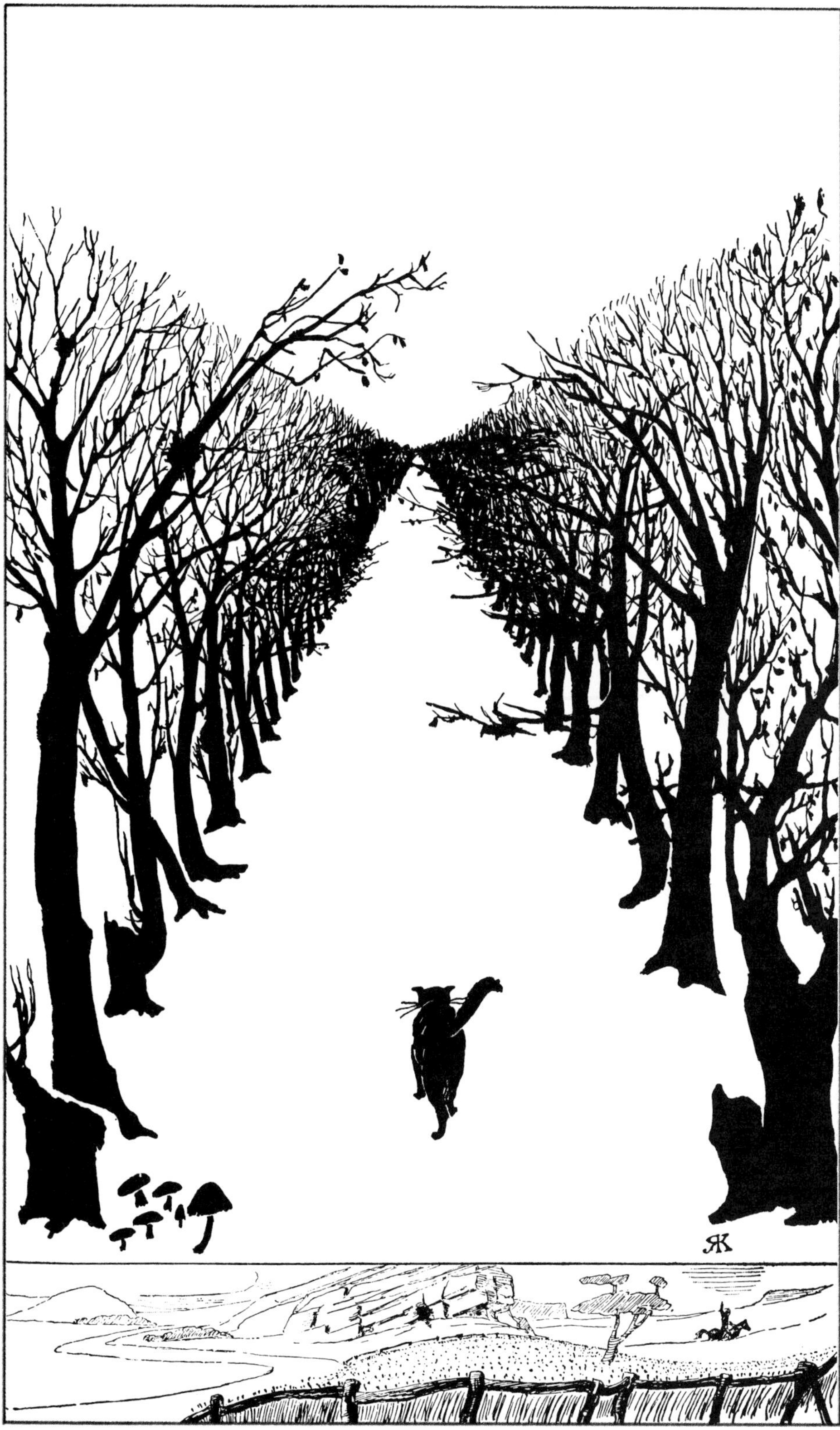

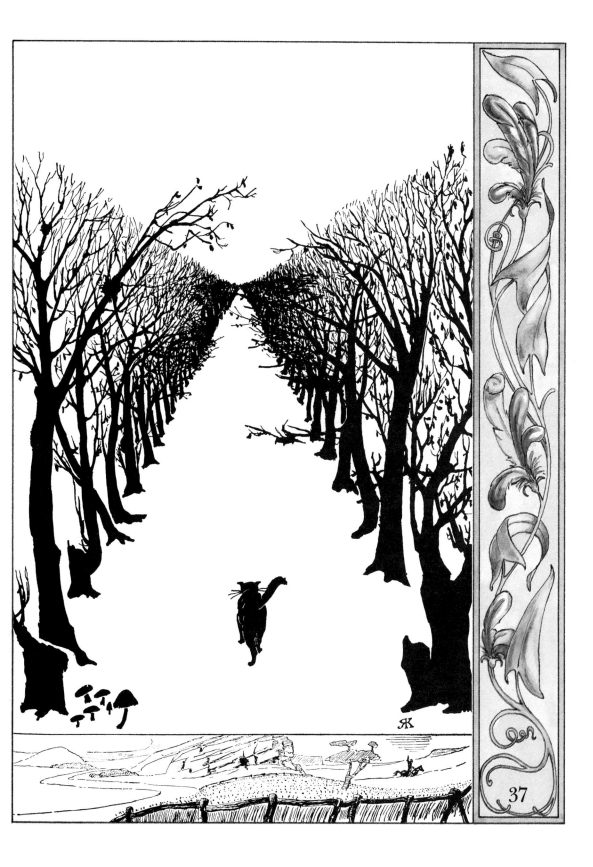

"Who Are You?"
Asked the Cat of the Bear

by

ELIZABETH COATSWORTH

"**W**ho are you?" asked the cat of the bear.
"I am a child of the wood.
I am strong with rain-shedding hair.
I hunt without fear for my food.
The others behold me and quail."
Said the cat, "You are lacking a tail."

"What can you do?" asked the cat.
"I can climb for the honey I crave.
  In the fall when I'm merry and fat
  I seek out a suitable cave
  And sleep till I feel the spring light."
  Said the cat, "Can you see in the night?"

Said the cat, "I sit by man's fire,
But I am much wilder than you.
I do the thing I desire
And do nothing I don't want to do.
I am small, but then, what is that?
My spirit is great," said the cat.

Aladdin and the Wonderful Lamp
from the
ARABIAN NIGHTS

Long ago, in a land far away, there lived a boy named Aladdin. His father had died. His mother worked hard at her spinning wheel. But they were still very poor.

One day a stranger came up to Aladdin at the market square. "Are you not the son of the baker of this town?" he asked.

"Indeed I am," said Aladdin. "But my father died a long time ago."

At this, the stranger cried out, "Oh, no! My poor dear brother! I made this long trip to see him again. But I am too late. Now you, his son, must take his place in my heart."

He gave Aladdin two pieces of gold.

"Take these to your mother," he said. "Tell
her I will visit tomorrow."

Aladdin ran home. He told his mother all
about the newly found uncle.

"How strange!" she said. "Your father
never told me he had a brother. But the
gold is welcome. Besides, it would be good for
you to learn from your uncle how to make
your living."

Now this stranger was not really Aladdin's uncle. He was really a wicked magician from another land. But Aladdin and his mother had no idea of this.

The stranger came to visit the next day. He brought Aladdin fine clothes. After dinner he led Aladdin outside the town gates. "I will take you to some beautiful gardens," he said. "And I will show you something wonderful indeed."

They walked through a long valley. Then they reached a pile of rocks at the foot of a mountain.

"Bring me some wood, Aladdin," said the magician. "I am going to make a fire."

Aladdin did as he was told.

"Good," said the man. "Now stand back. Keep well behind me."

He waved a red cloth over the fire and said some strange words.

All at once the rocks moved. The ground shook and opened in front of them. In the hole, Aladdin could see a square stone with a ring in the middle of it.

He turned to run. But the magician grabbed him and gave him a blow that knocked him down.

"Why did you hit me, Uncle?" cried Aladdin. "What have I done?"

"As yet, nothing!" shouted the magician. "But there is much that you *must* do! There is much that only you can do. I command you to stay here. You must not run away, and you must do just as I tell you."

Aladdin drew back in fear.

The magician pulled him closer to the square stone.

"See the ring that is in the middle of that stone," the magician went on. "It is written that only you can grab that ring and lift the stone. Below lies a treasure which is meant to be yours."

When he heard the word *treasure,* Aladdin forgot his fears. He grabbed the ring and pulled. The stone came up in his hand. Below, he saw some steps leading down to a door.

"Go through that door," said the magician. "You will find yourself in a beautiful garden. Walk on until you come to the far gate. There by the gate you will see a little old lamp. Bring that lamp back to me."

He took a ring from his finger. "Put this on," he told Aladdin. "It will keep you safe. Remember, you are meant to be richer than a king. But first you must bring me that lamp."

Aladdin walked down the steps. He opened the door and hurried to the gate.

Yes, there was the lamp. It was small and very old. It would never have caught his eye if he had not been sent for it. Aladdin put it deep in the pocket of his robe.

On his way back he looked more closely at the stones on the garden paths. How they sparkled! Each was as beautiful as a stone in a ring. And what a rainbow of colors! They were bright red and orange and green. Aladdin stuffed his pockets full.

When he reached the steps, the magician called to him. "Hurry! Bring up the lamp. Hand it to me."

"I can't until I am outside," said Aladdin. "It is in the pocket of my robe. All of the sparkling stones that I picked up from the garden path are on top of it. Help me up. My robe is heavy."

But the magician thought Aladdin was trying to trick him.

He thought Aladdin meant to keep the lamp. "You dog!" he cried. "Give me the lamp or die!"

Aladdin drew back, frightened at the change in the way the magician was acting. He knew that a real uncle would never have spoken to him that way. "Who are you?" he asked, his voice shaking.

"You will never know," the magician said darkly. He waved his hand and the square stone fell back into place.

Aladdin was trapped. For two days he stayed in the dark, beating on the stone and shouting. Again and again he tried to lift the stone. But it was no use.

At last he thought of the ring.

The magician had said it would keep him safe. He rubbed it.

At once a huge genie rose up from the ring. He said in a voice of thunder:

"I am the genie of the ring.
For you, I must do anything."

"Get me out of this place," cried Aladdin. "Take me to my home."

No sooner had he spoken than he found himself at home. Aladdin told his mother what had passed. He showed her the lamp and the stones from the garden. Then he asked for some food.

"I have nothing to eat in the house," she said, "and no money for food."

"I will sell the lamp," said Aladdin.

It looked so dirty that his mother wondered who would buy it. "It will sell better if you clean it," she said.

47

So Aladdin started to
rub it with a cloth.

Smoke rose from the lamp. A
shape rolled out of the smoke.
It was another genie, bigger and more
frightening than the genie of the ring.
Its voice filled the room.

"My power is great on sea and land.
The lamp makes your
wish my command."

"Bring us food," Aladdin commanded.

The genie brought forth food fit for a
king—rich meats, fine fruits, sweet cakes,
and candy. The food was piled high on
gold dishes.

In the days to come, they sold the gold
dishes, one by one. So Aladdin and his
mother were no longer poor. They lived well,
and this went on until he was a young man.

One day Aladdin heard the Sultan's guard shouting a message up and down the streets.

"People of the city," he cried. "Our Sultan commands that you go inside your houses. Close the doors and windows. The Sultan's daughter will pass by here. Her beauty is great, but any man who sets eyes upon her must die."

Hearing this, Aladdin closed the door of his house. But he left a crack in one window. As the Sultan's daughter passed, he was able to see her, just for a second.

49

But in that second, he fell in love. From then on, he could think of nothing but her.

He told his mother, "If I cannot win the hand of the Sultan's daughter, I do not wish to live."

"You are not a prince," said his mother. "If you ask to marry the princess, our Sultan will have your head cut off. You should not even think such thoughts."

"But I have riches to lay at the princess's feet," said he. "Remember the lamp, Mother. And remember the beautiful sparkling stones I brought back from the strange garden. You must help me. Take a little basket of the beautiful stones to the Sultan for his daughter. Tell him I wish to marry her."

The next day Aladdin's mother stood in the long line of people who hoped to see the Sultan. When it was her turn, she dropped to her knees before him.

"Good woman, tell me what you want," he said.

But Aladdin's mother was so frightened that she could not speak.

She had kept the basket hidden in the folds of her robe. Now she pulled out the basket and placed the beautiful stones before the Sultan.

The stones sparkled so brightly that the Sultan put his hand over his eyes. "What riches!" he said in wonder. "No eye has ever seen such beauty! But why are you bringing me such a treasure, good woman?"

"These stones are a present for your daughter from my son," she said.

"He wishes to marry the princess," she went on. "I told him to forget such a wild idea. But he can think of nothing else."

The Sultan picked up a sparkling red stone. He turned it to catch the light. "Does your son have more treasures, such as this stone?" he asked.

The woman nodded.

"Then I may give some thought to your son's wish," said the Sultan. "After all, who could be more fit to marry the princess than the richest man in the country? Tell your son to stand before me tomorrow."

The Sultan smiled. "He must bring a hundred followers, and each of them must carry a basket of treasures."

Aladdin's mother hurried home. She told her son what had taken place. At once he rubbed the lamp.

Just as before, the genie came forth.

"My power is great on sea and land.
     The lamp makes your wish my command."

"Make me ready to meet the Sultan,"
Aladdin said. By the next morning, all was
as he wished. He was richly robed. Riding on
a fine horse, he led his hundred followers to
the Sultan.

When the Sultan saw the treasures, he
was happy indeed. "Any king on earth would
be happy to have you for a son," he said to
Aladdin. "You may marry my daughter at
once."

"Before I make the princess my wife, I
must build a castle fit for her," said Aladdin.
"She will want to be close to you, so it should
be near your castle. If you will give me the
open square in the middle of our city, I will
build it there."

"Start at once," said the Sultan. "And let it
not take too long."

53

That night, Aladdin called upon the genie of the lamp, and a beautiful castle was ready by the next morning.

"Only by magic could this be done in one night," thought the Sultan. "But Aladdin's magic will make my daughter the richest princess on earth."

So Aladdin and the princess were married.

But before a year had passed, the wicked magician who had said he was Aladdin's uncle came again to the city.

He stayed in hiding until Aladdin went away on a hunting trip. Then he set about getting the magic lamp for himself. The magician bought some new lamps. He put them in a basket and went to the castle, calling, "New lamps for old! New lamps for old!"

The princess heard him and looked out the window. She laughed. "What kind of a fool would give somebody a new lamp for an old one?" she asked.

One of her women said, "Princess, there is a little old lamp in the closet. Is it your wish that I should take it to the man? Then we could see if he really means what he is saying."

The idea made the princess laugh. "Yes," she said. "Do so. Let us see what will happen."

The magician smiled a wicked smile when the woman handed the lamp to him. He knew it was the magic lamp. Quickly he gave the woman all of his new lamps. Then he rubbed the treasure he had wanted so long.

The genie came forth and stood ready to do whatever the magician commanded. "I want Aladdin's castle," he cried. "Take it, and everyone in it, back to my country. And take me there too, at once."

No sooner had he said the words than it was done.

The next day, the Sultan went to visit his daughter, but no castle was there. "What has happened!" he cried. "How can this be? Where is my daughter? Aladdin must answer for this."

He called his men. "Bring Aladdin back from his hunting trip," he commanded. "Bring him before me at once."

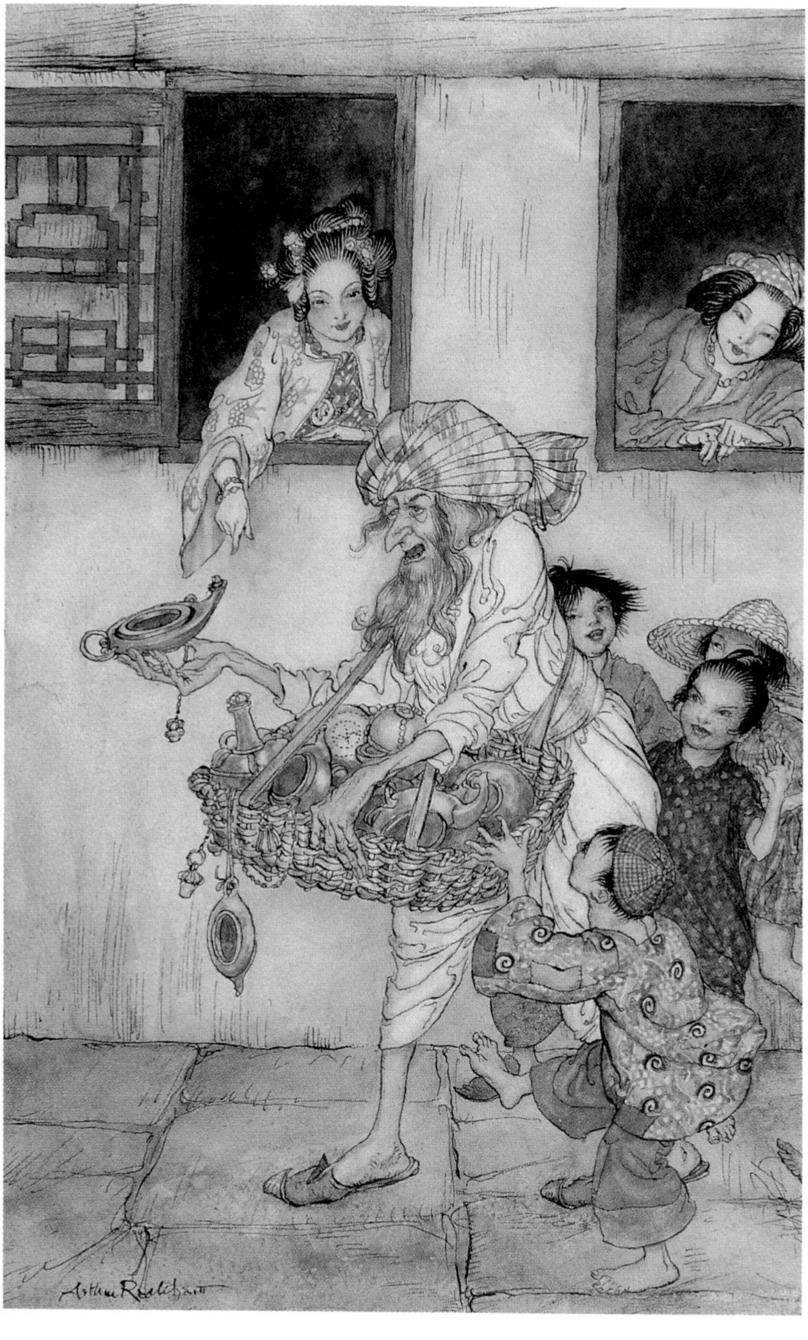
Arthur Rackham

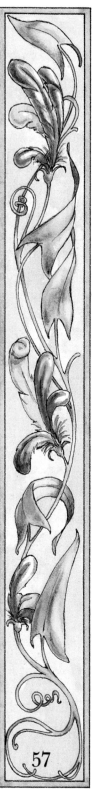

Aladdin was brought to where his castle had stood. When he saw that it was gone, he knew the magician must have returned.

"Bring my daughter back," the Sultan commanded, "or I will have your head cut off. The castle was built by your magic. Now you have moved it by your magic. But I care not for the castle. I care for my daughter. Return her here. She is my greatest treasure."

"Oh, King of the Ages, it was not I who moved the castle away. I do not know where the princess is. You have lost your daughter, but I have lost my wife. She is the love of my life, the moon of my being. If I cannot find her, I have no wish to live. Please give me three days to look for her."

"You have three days to bring her back," said the Sultan.

Aladdin went to his mother's house. He closed himself in a room and rubbed the ring.

At once the genie of the ring rose before him. "For the love of Allah," cried Aladdin. "Bring back my wife."

"That I cannot do," said the genie. "The power of the lamp is greater than the power of the ring."

Aladdin held his head in his hands. "Then take me to my wife," he commanded.

And there he was.

His wife fell into his arms. "I must hide you," she said. "The magician will kill you." She told Aladdin how the magician got the lamp.

"Where does he keep the magic lamp?" asked Aladdin.

"He carries it in his robe," she answered. "Each night I must tell him stories until he falls asleep. Last night I caught sight of the lamp in his robe."

"Tonight I will hide in your closet," said Aladdin. "When he falls asleep, I will cut off his head. Then the lamp will be ours again, and we can return to the land of your father."

And so the magician met his end, and Aladdin and his princess returned to the Sultan. There they lived happily and had many beautiful children.

Of course, they took the lamp with them and used its magic to do good for the rest of their days.

The Duck

by

OGDEN NASH

Behold the duck.
It does not cluck.
A cluck it lacks.
It quacks.

It is especially fond
Of a puddle or pond.
And when it dines or sups
It bottoms ups.

61

These two wise old sayings seem to be about birds, and they are true of birds. But aren't they also true of people?

Read these two proverbs from *Don Quixote* by Miguel Cervantes.

Birds of a Feather

by MIGUEL CERVANTES

Birds of a feather flock together.

A Bird in the Hand

by MIGUEL CERVANTES

A bird in the hand is worth two in the bush.

The Last Word of a Bluebird

(As Told to a Child)

by

ROBERT FROST

As I went out, a Crow
In a low voice said, "Oh,
I was looking for you.
How do you do?

I just came to tell you
To tell Lesley (will you?)
That her little bluebird
Wanted me to bring word
That the north wind last night
That made the stars bright
Almost made him cough
His tail feathers off.

He just had to fly!
But he sent her Good-by.
And perhaps in the spring
He would come back and sing."

A Bird Came down the Walk

by

EMILY DICKINSON

A bird came down the walk.
He did not know I saw.
He bit an angleworm in halves
And ate the fellow, raw.

And then he drank a dew
From a convenient grass,
And then hopped sidewise to the wall
To let a beetle pass.

The Pied Piper of Hamelin

from a European folktale retold by

JOSEPH JACOBS

Hamelin is a sleepy little town. But sleepy as it is now, it was once noisy enough. And what made the noise? Rats! Big rats and little rats! Old rats and young rats! Squeaking and running about, all day and all night! The town was once so full of them that it was not fit to live in.

Those rats ate their way into each house and barn. Every morning the people would find rats in their boots and shoes. At night the mothers and fathers could not sleep. They feared that the rats would bite their babies.

Why didn't the good people of the town have cats? Well, they did, and the cats had a fierce fight with the rats. But in the end the rats were too many for the cats, and the cats were pushed back.

Rat catchers?
Traps? Dogs? The
people of Hamelin
tried them all,
and nothing worked. Each day they were
faced with more and more rats.

The people of the town went to the Mayor.
"What shall we do?" asked one man.
"What can we try next?" said another.
The Mayor just shook his head. "I don't
know," he said.

One day a stranger came to the town. He
was tall with long arms and legs.

Every color in the rainbow could be seen in his clothes. He walked down the street, playing music on his pipe.

The people followed him. Soon he stood before the Mayor of Hamelin.

"I am called the Pied Piper," he began. "I am a fine rat catcher. I could see to it that not a rat was left to squeak in your town. Wouldn't that be a fine piece of work? What might you be willing to pay me for such help?"

The Mayor turned to the people. As much as they wanted the rats killed, they wanted to keep their money even more.

"Would you do it for two pieces of gold?" asked a woman.

The Pied Piper laughed. "No. Not for two. Not for ten. You must pay me a hundred pieces of gold, or I'll be on my way."

The Mayor frowned. Some of the people turned away. But after more talk, they made a bargain with him for a hundred pieces of gold.

The Piper laid his pipe to his lips. The music sounded through street and house. With each note, you might have seen a strange sight, for out of every hole came rats. Black rats and gray rats! Young rats and old rats! None were too big and none were too little to follow him.

Up Silver Street he went, and down Gold Street. At the end of Gold Street was the river. As he walked along, playing his pipe, the people watched without saying a word.

As for getting near him, there were too many rats. And now that he was at the bank of the river, he stepped into a boat.

As he headed into deep water, all the rats followed, splashing after him. On and on he played, into the night. He played his music until every rat from the town had drowned in the river.

The next day he stood before the Mayor.

"There is not a rat left in the town of Hamelin," said the Pied Piper. "So I will take my hundred pieces of gold and be on my way."

71

The Mayor looked at the people. They shook their heads.

"Come, my good man," said the Mayor. "A hundred is too much. We do not have a lot of money. Each man and woman in our town would have to help pay you. Will you not take ten pieces of gold?"

He added, "That would be good pay for the little work you did."

"You and your people promised me a hundred pieces of gold," said the Pied Piper. "If I were you, I would pay quickly, or you may find that I can play many kinds of music. There are some kinds that you would not wish for me to play."

"Are you trying to frighten us?" asked the Mayor. "The rats are gone, so you may do whatever you will. We will not pay you at all."

"Very well," said the Piper, and he smiled a quiet smile. He picked up his pipe. Now there was music full of happy laughter and play.

The men and women walked away. But from the schoolrooms and the play rooms, children ran out.

Every child in the town followed the Piper's call. Dancing, laughing, singing, they moved up Gold Street. Holding hands, they went up Silver Street. And past Silver Street lay the green forest that led to the hills.

All the children followed the Piper through the forest to the side of a hill. It opened a little. The Piper went in, and so did the children. Then it closed again, and the Piper's music was heard no more.

A little boy who had hurt his foot was trailing far behind. He saw what happened, and he went back to Hamelin and told the people.

They ran to the hill, but they could find no sign of an opening so they did not believe him.

They waited for their children to return. But watch and wait as they might, never again did they see their children, and never again did they set eyes on the Pied Piper.

• • • •

What became of the children? A hundred years later, people were still wondering. Some said that the Piper took them to his own land. Others said he led them into a country far from Hamelin where they grew up and had children of their own.

To this day, no one really knows. But when the beginnings of a town are hidden in mystery, people wonder. And when a group seems to come out of nowhere, people guess.

And when people wonder and guess, the children of Hamelin come to mind.

The Pied Piper of Hamelin

excerpt from the poem by

ROBERT BROWNING

Rats!
They fought the dogs and killed the cats,
And bit the babies in the cradles,
And licked the soup from the cooks' own ladles,
Made nests inside men's Sunday hats,
And even spoiled the women's chats.

The Fisherman and His Wife

by the

BROTHERS GRIMM

There was once a fisherman who lived with his wife. They had a little hut by the sea. Each day he went out to catch fish.

One day when he pulled up his line, he found a great flounder on the hook.

The flounder said to him, "Fisherman, listen to me. Let me go. I am not a real fish. I am really a prince, and I have great powers.

But I am under a spell. If you cooked me, I would not be good to eat. So please put me back in the water again, and let me swim away."

"Well," said the fisherman. "No need of so many words about the matter. Since you can talk, I would not feel right cooking you, and I could not bring myself to eat you. Do swim away."

He put him back into the clear water. Then the fisherman went home to his wife.

"Well, husband," she said. "Did you catch anything today?"

"No," said the man. "Nothing but a flounder, but he said he was a prince with great powers, so I let him go again."

"Just like that?" she asked. "You let him go without asking for anything? Didn't you ask for a wish?"

"No," he said. "What should I wish for?"

"Oh, dear," said the wife. "It is so awful to live in this ugly little hut. You might have wished for a pretty house. Go again and call him. Tell him we want a house. I think he will give it to us. Go and be quick."

When the fisherman went back, the sea was green and yellow, and not so clear. He stood and said,

"Man, oh man, if man you be,
    Or flounder, flounder, in the sea,
    Such a greedy wife I've got,
    For she wants what I do not."

The flounder came swimming up. "Now, then, what does she want?" he asked.

"Oh," said the man. "When I caught you, my wife says I should have wished for something. She does not want to live in our little hut. She wants a pretty house."

"Go home," said the flounder. "She has the house."

So the man went home. He found, instead of his hut, a pretty house. His wife was at the door.

She took him by the hand. "Come in," she said. "Isn't this fine?"

So he went in, and there was a nice front room and a kitchen full of food. In the back was a little yard with chickens and ducks. There was a small garden to the side of the house.

"Look at all we have now," said his wife. "Was I not right to make you go back?"

The man smiled. "With all this, we can be happy for the rest of our lives."

"We will see about that," said the wife.

All went well for a week. Then the wife said, "Look here, husband. This house is too small. I think the flounder had better get us a larger house. I would like to live in a stone castle, so go to your fish and tell him to send us a castle."

"Oh, my dear wife," said the fisherman. "This house is good enough. What do we want a castle for?"

"I want one," said the wife. "Go along now. The flounder can give us one."

"Now, wife," said the man. "The flounder gave us this house. I do not like to go to him again. He may be angry."

"Go along," said the wife. "He might just as well give us a castle. Do as I say."

The man sighed. "It is not the right thing to do," he said to himself, but he went back to the sea.

The water was dark blue, not green and yellow as before. He said,

> "Man, oh man, if man you be,
> Or flounder, flounder, in the sea,
> Such a greedy wife I've got,
> For she wants what I do not."

"Now, then, what does she want?" asked the flounder.

"Oh," said the man, half frightened. "She wants to live in a large stone castle."

"Go home," said the flounder. "She is now standing at the door."

So the man went home. When he got there, in place of the house was a big stone castle. His wife took him by the hand and said, "Let us go in."

With that, he went in with her. In the castle was a great hall. The rooms had golden chairs and tables. At the back was a field for horses.

The garden of the castle was full of beautiful flowers.

"There!" said the wife. "Is this not beautiful?"

"Oh, yes," said the man. "We can live in this fine castle and be happy for the rest of our lives."

"We will see about that," said the wife.

The next morning, she woke up first. She looked out and saw the beautiful lands far off from her castle.

"Husband, get up," she said. "Look out the window. Just think how fine it would be if I could be queen of all those lands! Go to your fish. Tell him I want to be queen."

"Now, wife," said the man. "What do you want to be queen for? I could not ask him such a thing."

"Why not?" said the wife. "You must go all the same. I must be queen."

"Oh, wife," said the man. "The fish really cannot do that for you. Do be happy with what he has given you."

"Husband," said she. "I'll have no more words about it. You must do as I say, so go along."

The man went, but he was very much put out that his wife should want to be queen.

"It is not the right thing to do. It is not at all the right thing," thought the man. He did not want to go, and yet he went all the same.

When he came to the sea, the water was black and thick. A great wind was blowing, and it grew very dark. He called the fish.

"Man, oh man, if man you be,
   Or flounder, flounder, in the sea,
   Such a greedy wife I've got,
   For she wants what I do not."

"What is it now?" said the fish.

"Oh, dear," said the man. "My wife wants to be queen."

"Go home," said the fish. "She is queen."

85

So the man went home. He found knights all around his castle, and he saw his wife with a golden crown on her head.

The man went up to her and said, "Well, wife, so now you are queen."

"Yes," she said. "Now I am queen."

He went and sat down and had a good look at her. Then he said, "Well, now, wife, there is nothing more left to be, now that you are queen."

"We will see about that," she said.

That night she could not get to sleep for thinking about what she wanted next. She turned from side to side the whole night through. At last she got up and sat by the window to see the sun come up.

As it came up, she said, "Ah, I have it! What if I should make the sun and moon come up? Husband, get up! Go to your fish. Tell him I want power over the sun and moon."

The man opened his eyes. "Oh, wife! What did you say?"

"Get up! Get up," she told him. "If I cannot get the power to make the sun and moon come up, I shall never be happy. Go to the fish and tell him so."

"Now, wife," he said. "How can I ask him such a thing? It is asking too much."

"Go!" said his wife. "Do as I tell you. I am queen. You are only my husband, so you must go. I will wait no longer. Go at once."

Now the man was frightened. Off he went into a heavy rain. The wind was blowing fiercely. Houses and trees were blown down. Rocks fell into the sea. He cried out,

"Man, oh man, if man you be,
   Or flounder, flounder, in the sea,
   Such a greedy wife I've got,
   For she wants what I do not."

"Well, what now?" asked the flounder.

"Oh, dear," said the man. "My wife wants power over the sun and moon."

"Go home," said the flounder. "You will find her in your old hut."

And there they are sitting to this very day.

A Wee Little Worm

by

JAMES WHITCOMB RILEY

A wee little worm in a hickory nut
Sang, happy as he could be,
"Oh, I live in the heart
    of the whole round world,
And it all belongs to me."

UNIT TWO

Here and There,
Then and Now

Swahili A B C

from

JAMBO MEANS HELLO

by

MURIEL FEELINGS

Swahili is spoken across more of Africa than any other language. There are no Q or X sounds in Swahili. So there are only 24 letters in the Swahili alphabet. Here are Swahili words for the letters A, B, and C.

A **arusi** is a wedding.
(ah-ROO-see)
When two people marry, everyone in
their village comes to the wedding.
There is drumming, dancing, and much
food for all.

B **baba** means father.
(BAH-bah)
Parents teach their children the things they will need to know when they are grown. The father teaches his sons to build the home and to make tools.

C **chakula** is food.
(cha-ĸoo-lah)
In villages the people grow most of their
food. Many families raise crops like corn,
green vegetables, fruits, and nuts.

95

At the Grandfather's

from

HEIDI

by

JOHANNA SPYRI

Heidi's Aunt Dete can no longer take care of her. She takes Heidi up the mountain to Grandfather's hut. Poor Heidi is dressed in all the clothes she owns, to save the trouble of carrying them. She is so hot that she takes off her thick red shawl and three dresses.

As soon as Heidi was left with her grandfather outside his hut in the hills, she started to look around. Her grandfather just sat on the bench in front of his little hut while she explored.

Near the hut she found the shed for his goats. She peeked into it. It was empty.

Then she found the tall trees behind the hut. The wind whistled through their branches. Heidi stood still and listened.

When the wind quieted down, she went back to her grandfather. She found him at the same place where she had left him. He was still sitting on the bench, not saying a word.

She placed herself in front of him, put her hands behind her, and looked at him.

"What is it?" her grandfather asked.

"I want to see what you have inside the hut," said Heidi.

"Come along then," he said. "And bring your bundle of clothes."

He rose and went into the hut. "You can put your things in the cupboard."

Heidi followed him into a good-sized room. In it were a table and a chair. In one corner was his bed. In another was the fireplace, with a big cooking pot hanging over it.

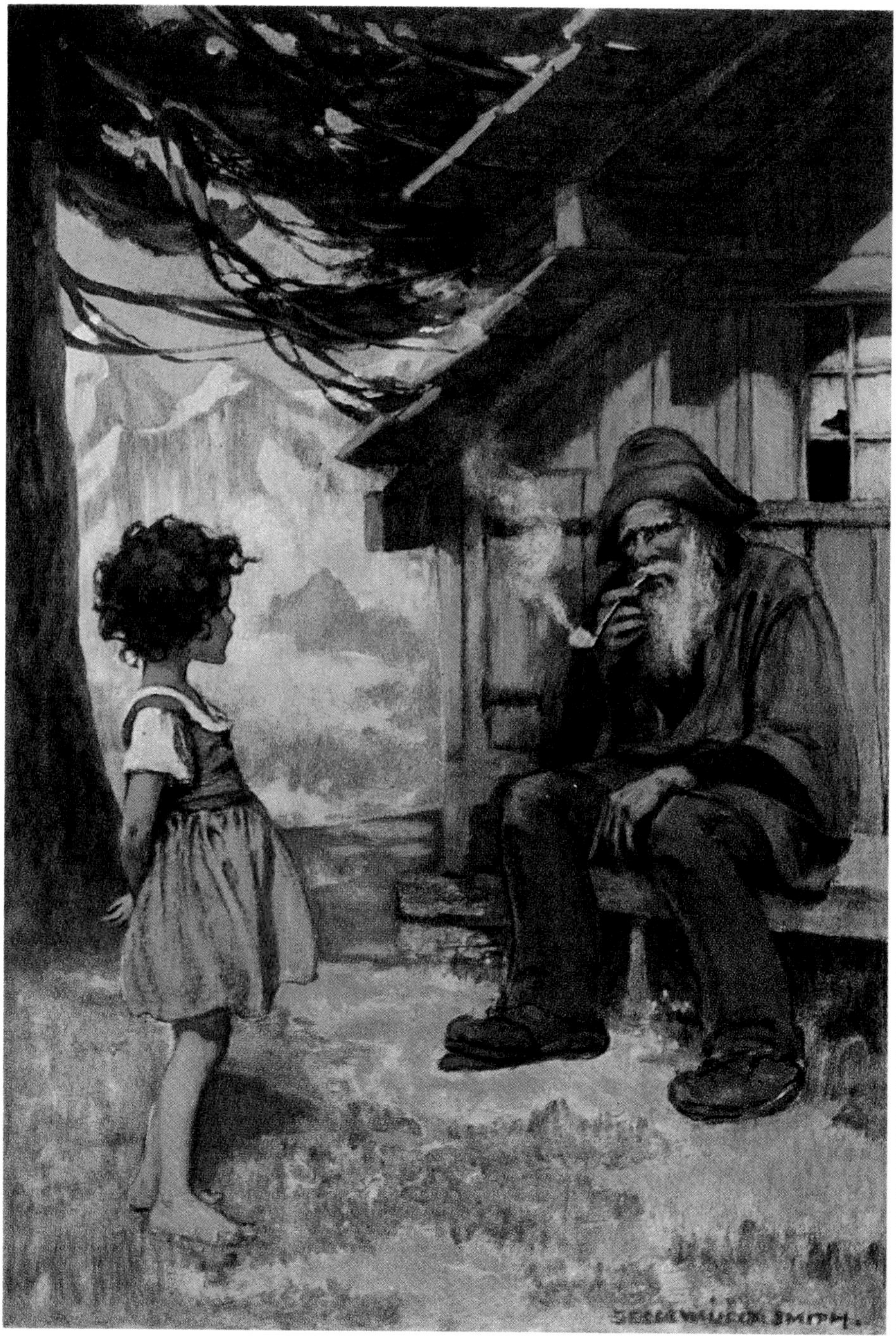

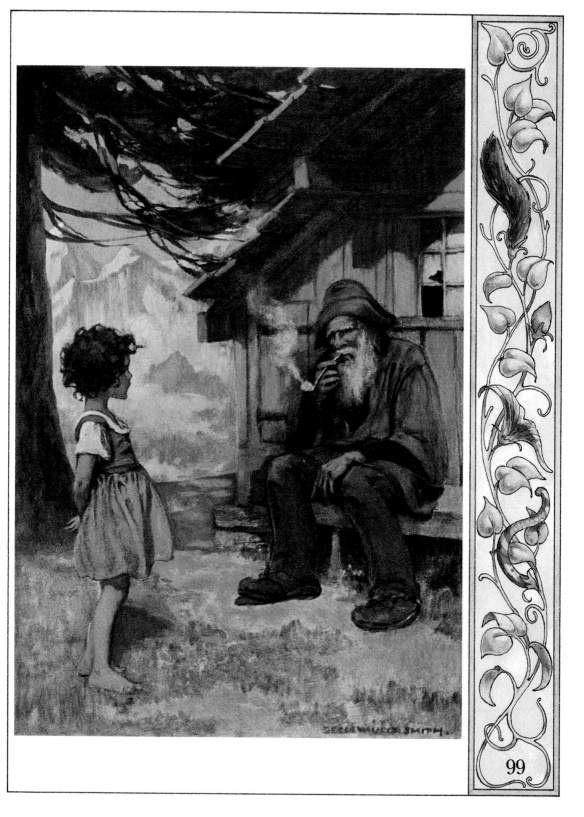

On the other side was a large door, which the grandfather opened. It was the cupboard. There were dishes and cups, bread, smoked meat, and cheese.

His shirts were stacked at the bottom. Everything he owned and needed was kept in this cupboard.

As soon as he opened the door, Heidi came running, carrying her bundle of clothes. She pushed them into the cupboard, in back of her grandfather's clothes.

Then she looked carefully around the room and said, "Where shall I sleep, Grandfather?"

"Wherever you like," he replied.

Heidi looked into every corner to see where would be the best place for her to sleep. In the corner by her grandfather's bed stood a little ladder, which led to the hayloft.

Heidi climbed the ladder. There lay a sweet-smelling pile of fresh hay.

Through a round window she could look far down into the valley below.

"I will sleep here," Heidi called down. "It is lovely! Just come and see how lovely it is here!"

"I know all about it," sounded from below.

"I am going to make a bed," called Heidi. She piled up some hay. "But you must bring a sheet, for the bed must have a sheet."

"Well, well," said the grandfather. He went to the cupboard and looked in. Then he pulled out a heavy cloth that might do for a sheet.

He came up the ladder and found that a very nice little bed had been made.

Heidi had put more hay at one end to make the head. It was placed in such a way that one could look from it straight out the round open window.

"That is made very nicely," said the grandfather. "Next comes the sheet.

But wait—" He took up more hay and piled
the bed higher, in order that the hard floor
might not be felt through it. "There. Now put
it on."

Then the two of them together spread
the sheet over the hay, and where it was too
long, Heidi tucked it under. Now it seemed
tight and smooth. Heidi stood looking at it
thoughtfully.

"We have forgotten one thing, Grandfather,"
she said.

"What is that?" he asked.

"The blanket. When we go to bed, we get
in between the sheet and the blanket."

"Is that so? But supposing I haven't any
blanket?" asked the old man.

"Oh, then it's no matter," said Heidi.
"We can take more hay for a blanket."
She was about to run to get more hay.
But her grandfather stopped her.

"Wait a minute," he said. He went down the ladder. Soon he came back with a heavy blanket.

"Isn't that better than hay?" he asked.

Heidi pulled the blanket over the bed. Then she looked at her new resting place and she smiled. "That is a fine blanket, and the whole bed is lovely. How I wish it were night so that I could lie down on it!"

"I think we might have something to eat first," said her grandfather. "What do you say?"

While getting her bed ready, Heidi had forgotten everything else. But now she felt very hungry.

She had taken nothing all day, except a piece of bread and a cup of milk in the morning. Then she had made the long trip to her grandfather's.

"Yes, I would like something to eat," she said.

103

"Well, let us go down," said the old man. He followed close upon Heidi's steps.

He went to the fireplace and built a bright fire. The old man held over the fire a large piece of cheese on the end of a long fork. He moved it this way and that, until it was golden yellow on all sides.

Heidi looked on with wide eyes. Then a new idea came to her mind. She jumped up, ran to the cupboard, and took things to the table.

When her grandfather brought over the toasted cheese, the table was set with dishes and cups. Heidi knew what would be needed. She had even cut the bread.

"That is right, to think of doing things yourself," said the grandfather. He put the cheese on the bread. "But there is something still needed. Where are you going to sit?"

The grandfather sat on the only chair.

Heidi ran over to the little three-legged stool, pulled it back, and sat down on it.

"Well, now you have a place to sit, only it is too low," said her grandfather. "Even in my chair you would be too short to reach the table. But now you must have something to eat anyway. So come."

After saying that, he rose from his chair. Then he pushed his chair close to the three-legged stool, so that Heidi had a table in front of her.

He put bread and a piece of the golden cheese on a dish on the chair. Then he filled Heidi's cup with milk and put it in front of her.

"Now eat," he said.

Her grandfather sat on the corner of the table and began his dinner.

Heidi picked up her cup and took a long drink of milk.

105

"Do you like the milk?" her grandfather asked.

"I never tasted such good milk before," answered Heidi.

"Then you must have some more," said her grandfather. He filled her cup again and placed it before her.

She began to eat her bread, after it had been spread with the toasted cheese, soft as butter. It tasted very good.

When they were finished, the grandfather went to his workbench. Heidi watched him closely as he cut some round sticks.

Then he shaped a board, made some holes in it and put the round sticks into them, and suddenly it was a stool like his own, only much higher. Heidi was wide-eyed with wonder as she saw his work.

"What is this, Heidi?" asked her grandfather.

"It is a stool for me, because it is so high.

You made it all at once," said Heidi, still surprised.

Evening was coming on. Heidi followed her grandfather outside to the goat shed. She watched as he spread fresh straw for the goats to sleep on. The wind was beginning to blow harder in the trees. It sounded beautiful in Heidi's ears.

"I must see to the goats soon," he said. "You go in and get ready for bed. Sleep well."

"Good night, Grandfather!" She danced into the hut and climbed up to her bed. Heidi fell asleep at once, as happy as if her bed were in a castle.

• • • •

You have just read how Heidi settled in with her grandfather in the Swiss Alps. But that is just the beginning of the story. There are many more adventures in the book *Heidi.*

André

by

GWENDOLYN BROOKS

I had a dream last night. I dreamed
I had to pick a mother out.
I had to choose a father too.
At first, I wondered what to do,
There were so many there, it seemed,
Short and tall and thin and stout.

But just before I sprang awake,
I knew what parents I would take.

And this surprised and made me glad:
They were the ones I always had!

Tom Feelings

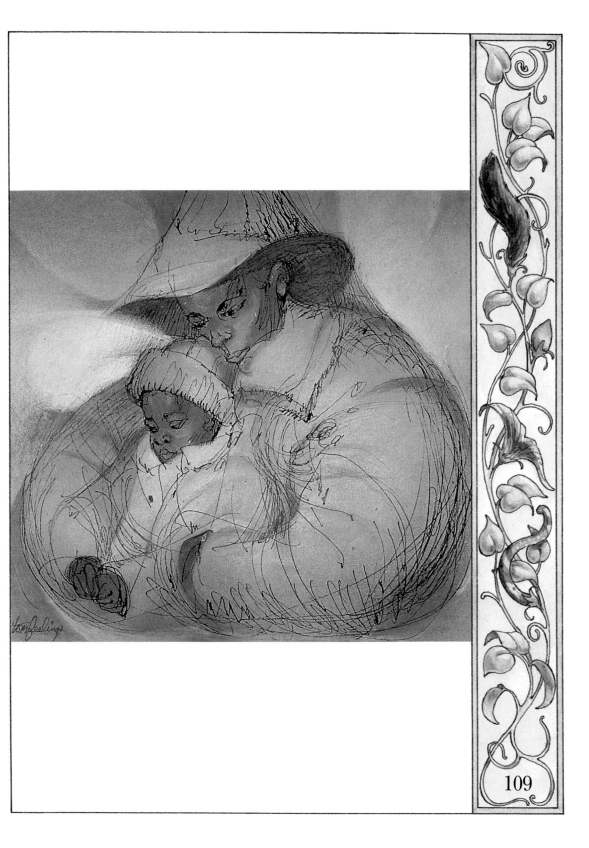

Coyote and Goat

a Mexican fable from Aesop

Columbus sailed to America in 1492. Not long after that, North America discovered Aesop's fables. A book of these well-known animal stories reached Mexico on a ship from Spain. The Indians of Mexico soon made the stories their own.

In Aesop's fables the fox is most often the tricky animal. But in the Mexican retellings, the coyote is the animal who plays tricks, as you will see in this fable.

One summer morning Coyote and Goat were walking together.

"What a hot day!" Goat said to Coyote. "How good it would be to have a long drink of water."

"There is a big well not far from here," said Coyote. "If we jump in, we can drink our fill."

Goat followed Coyote to the well, and in they jumped with a splash! They drank all the water they wanted.

Then Goat asked Coyote, "How are we going to get out of this well? I can't jump high enough to jump out."

"I know how to get out," said Coyote. "Let me show you. First I will climb on your back."

Goat stood still so that Coyote could get on his back.

"Now hold your head up high so that your horns stick out behind," said Coyote.

He used Goat's horns for his last steps to get to the top of the well. Then he jumped up onto the ground.

When Coyote was out, he looked down at Goat and laughed. "See, my friend," he said. "I told you I knew how to get out."

"But what about me?" said Goat.

"You?" said Coyote. "Why, you have learned a lesson."

**Before you get in, you need
to know how to get out.**

Hungry but Free

a Russian fable from Aesop

retold by

LEO TOLSTOY

here was once a wolf who was very hungry. He wandered by a farmyard one snowy morning. There he saw a dog finishing a big bowl of food.

The wolf trotted over to the dog. "Who gives you all that good food?" he asked.

"The farmer," said the dog.

"And what do you do for the farmer?" asked the wolf.

"I guard the farmyard at night," the dog replied.

"That is not a hard job to do for food," said the wolf. "In winter it is a very hard job to find food in the wilds. Some days I go hungry. Would the farmer give me food if I helped you guard the farmyard at night?"

"Oh, yes," said the dog. "The farmer feeds all his animals well. Come along. I'll take you to him."

As the wolf walked beside the dog, he noticed a bald patch on the dog's neck.

"Tell me something, my friend," said the wolf. "How did you come to lose that patch of hair from your neck?"

"My chain rubbed it away," said the dog. "During the day the farmer chains me to a tree, you see, and my chain is short and tight."

The wolf stopped. "I have changed my mind," he said. "I don't think I want to work for the farmer, even though he would feed me well. I will keep on hunting for my food in the wilds." And he trotted away.

**It is better to be hungry and free
than full and chained.**

My First Word

from

THE STORY OF MY LIFE

by

HELEN KELLER

The most important day I remember in all my life is the one on which my teacher, Anne Sullivan, came to me. It was the third of March 1887. I was six years and nine months old.

A sickness had left me without sight or hearing when I was not yet two years old. So my world had long been dark and still. I could not see or listen or speak.

But that day in March 1887, I felt that something was about to happen. From my mother's signs and the hurrying around in the house, I guessed that someone was coming. So I went to the door, slipped outside, and waited on the steps.

I felt footsteps, coming from the gate. I stretched out my hand. Someone took it. I was caught up and held close in the arms of someone new in my young life. Miss Anne Sullivan! My teacher! She had come to open the world for me and to love me.

The morning after my teacher came, she led me into her room and gave me a doll. When I had played with it a little while, Miss Sullivan slowly spelled into my hand the word "d-o-l-l."

I was at once interested in this finger play. I tried to move my fingers to make different shapes, just as my teacher had done. But I did not know that I was spelling a word. I didn't even know what "a word" was. I was just copying my teacher in a monkeylike way.

In the days that followed, I learned to spell other words. Among them were "hat" and "cup," and a few verbs like "sit," "stand," and "walk."

But my teacher had been with me many weeks before I understood that everything had a name.

One day, while I was playing with my new doll, Miss Sullivan handed me my old doll. She spelled d-o-l-l into my hand for both dolls, trying to make me understand. But I did not understand. Again and again she tried.

I became angry. So I grabbed the new doll and dashed it upon the floor. I was pleased when I felt the pieces of the broken doll at my feet. In the still, dark world in which I lived, I was angry much of the time.

My teacher brushed the broken pieces of the doll to one side of the fireplace. Then she brought me my hat. So I knew I was going out into the warm sunshine. This thought, if an idea without words can be called a thought, made me happy enough to hop and run.

We walked down the path to the well. Someone was pumping water. My teacher placed my hand under the pump.

As the cool stream ran over one hand, she spelled into the other hand the word "water," first slowly, then faster. I stood still, my whole being fixed on the touch of her fingers.

Suddenly I felt a flash of thought, of understanding. Somehow the magic of language was coming to me. I knew then that w-a-t-e-r meant the wonderful cool something that was streaming over my hand. That living word gave me light, hope, joy, and set me free.

As we returned to the house, everything I touched seemed wonderful. That was because I saw everything with the strange new sight that had come to me.

I learned a great many new words that day. I do not remember what they all were. But I do know that "mother," "father," and "teacher" were some of them.

It would have been hard to find a happier child than I was as I lay in my bed at the close of that day. I lived over the joys it had brought me, and for the first time, I longed for a new day to come.

The White Horse

by

D. H. LAWRENCE

The youth walks up to the white horse,
    to put its halter on
and the horse looks at him in silence.
They are so silent they are in another world.

Jason and the Centaur

by

CHARLES KINGSLEY

Long ago in Greece there lived a young man named Jason. He lived in the forest with his teacher, who was a centaur. Centaurs were fine creatures, tall and strong and very wise. Each centaur had the head and arms of a man and the body and legs of a horse.

One day Jason asked the centaur a question. "Good teacher of mine," he started. "Long have you told me that I am meant to be king of a land far from here. Is it not time for me to start traveling toward that land?"

The centaur smiled. "You must win many battles before you can be king. You will need the help of the gods and goddesses on Mount Olympus. Many strong men will want to stop you."

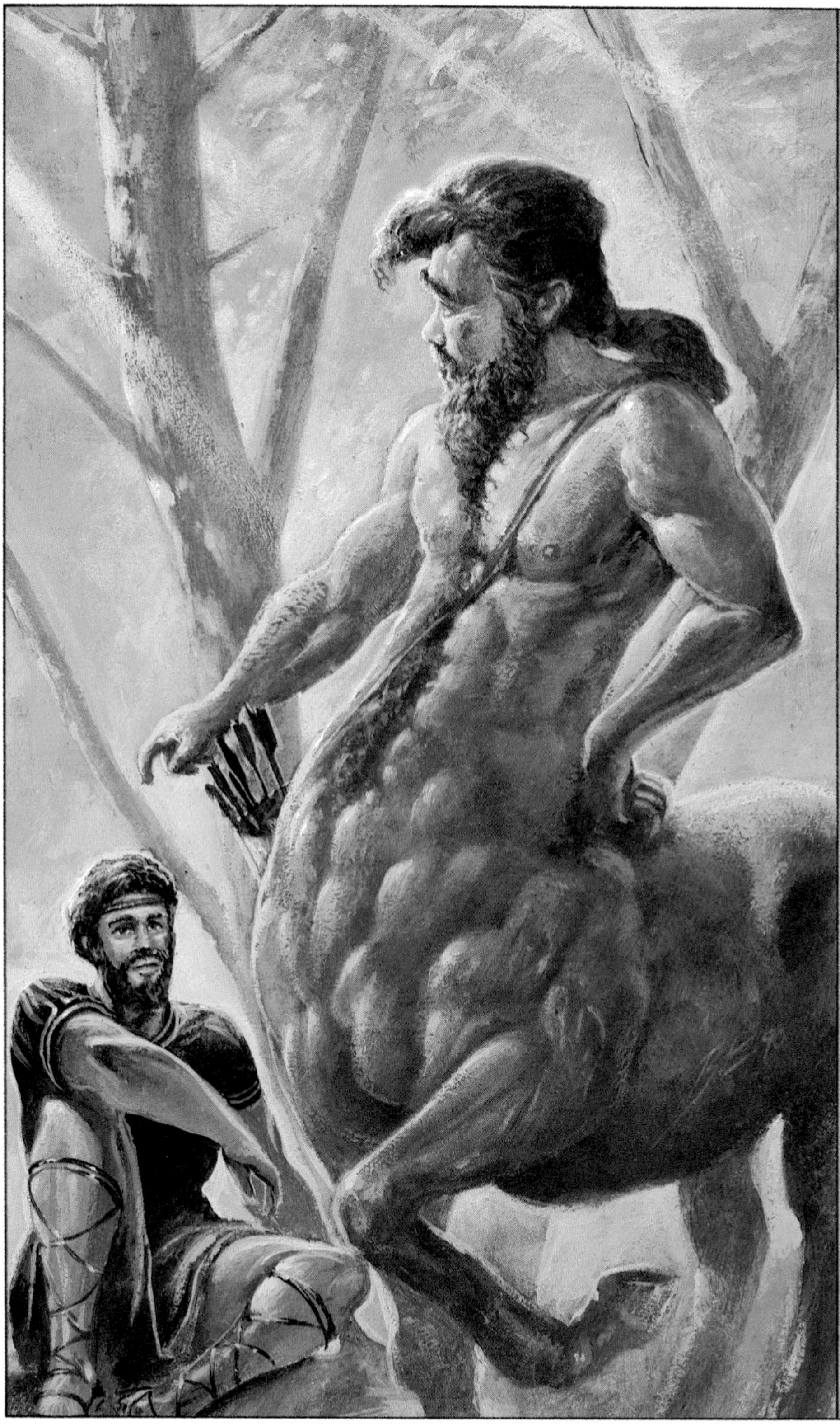

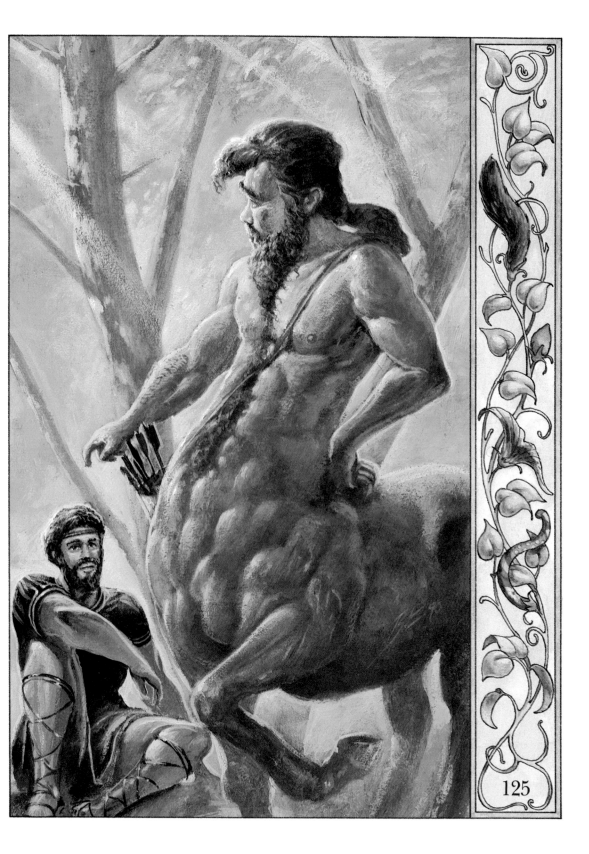

"I am ready to do battle with all who cross me," said Jason. "You have trained me well."

"You are *too* ready to do battle," said the centaur. "Yet it is time for you to go forth, but promise me two things."

"I will promise," said Jason.

"Speak sharply to no one that you may meet," said the centaur. "And stand by the word which you shall speak."

Jason promised.

He left the forest. Soon he came to a river roaring with a summer flood.

On the bank of the river sat a woman. She was old and gray.

When she saw Jason, she called out to him, "Will you carry me across the flood?"

Jason was just about to step into the river and try to make his way across. The roaring waters rushed quickly along, carrying rocks down from the higher banks.

126

The old woman called again. "I need help, young man," she cried. "Please carry me over the flood."

Jason was about to answer her sharply. He was not sure he could get himself across! But then he remembered his promise to the centaur. He would speak sharply to no one.

So he said, "In the name of Hera, Queen of Mount Olympus, I will carry you. But hold on. We may both be washed away in this flood."

The old woman leaped upon his back. She was quick and heavy, far heavier than he had thought she would be.

At the first step, the water came to his knees.

At the second step, it splashed his belt. His feet slipped on the stones. But he went on, sliding and panting and almost falling.

The old woman cried, "Fool! My shoes are wet! Be careful where you step. Are you making fun of carrying a poor old woman?"

Jason had half a mind to drop her. But the centaur's words stayed in his mind. So he said only, "Sorry, my lady."

At last he climbed out of the wild water onto the far bank, and he set the old woman down on the ground.

Jason lay panting in the grass, too tired to move. He looked at the old woman and waited for her to thank him.

But as he looked, she grew fairer than all women on earth, and she grew taller than all men on earth. She looked down on him with great soft eyes.

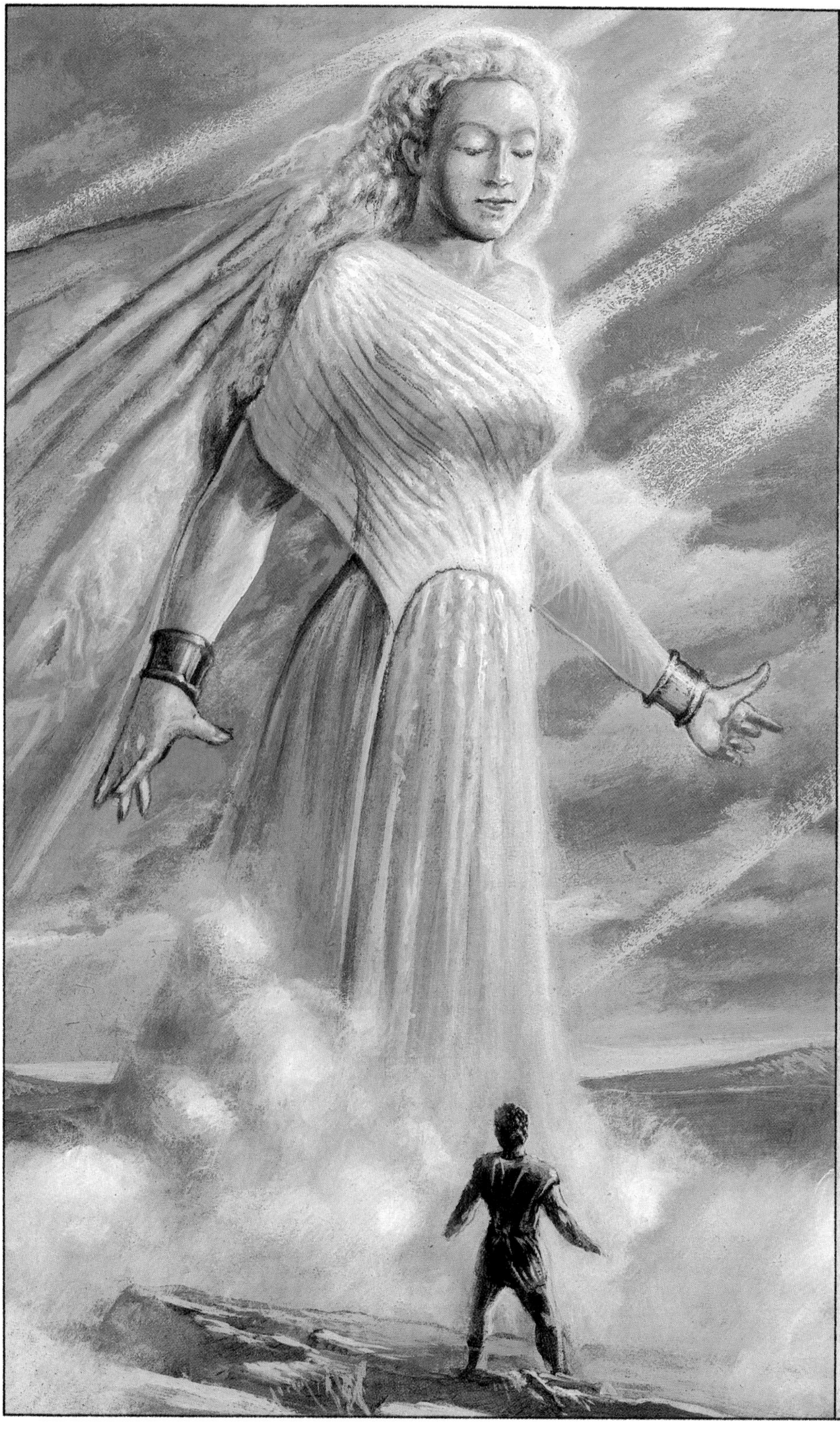

Jason fell upon his knees.

She spoke. "I am Hera, Queen of the gods and goddesses of Mount Olympus. As you have done for me, so I will do for you. Call on me in your hour of need."

Then she rose from the earth like a tall white cloud, and she floated to the top of Mount Olympus.

Then a great fear fell on Jason, knowing he had thought of dropping her.

But after a while he grew light of heart. He thought happily of his old teacher and said, "Surely the centaur was wise. He guessed what would come to pass. That is why he made me promise to speak sharply to no one and to keep my word."

In Time of Silver Rain

by

LANGSTON HUGHES

In time of silver rain
The earth
Puts forth new life again.
Green grasses grow
And flowers lift their heads.
And over all the plain
The wonder spreads
    Of life,
    Of life,
    Of life!

Hansel and Gretel

A PLAY

adapted from a fairy tale by the

BROTHERS GRIMM

People in the Play
  The narrator
  The woodcutter
  His wife
  His son, Hansel
  His daughter, Gretel
  The witch

Narrator   Near a great forest lived a very poor woodcutter and his wife and his two children.

Woodcutter   What will become of us? How can we feed the children when we don't have food for ourselves? There is nothing left to eat but a few pieces of bread.

Wife   I'll tell you what we should do. Let's take the children early in the morning into the forest. Then we will leave them alone. They will never find their way home.

Woodcutter   No, wife! I cannot do that. I cannot leave my children in the forest. The wild animals would eat them.

Wife   Oh, you fool! Then we will *all* go hungry. None of us can live without food. But if the children were not here, there would be a bit more food for us to eat.

Narrator   His wife would give him no rest. So the next day he took Hansel and Gretel into the forest. He left them there. But they found their way home. So he had to take them into the forest again. This time, they could not find their way back.

Gretel   How shall we ever get out of this forest? We have been walking for such a long time.

133

Hansel Do not worry, little sister. We'll find our way soon.

Gretel It is so hard to keep going with nothing to eat. Please, Hansel, let's rest.

Hansel No, let's go a little farther. I think I see a house up ahead.

Gretel Yes. It is a house, but what a strange one! It looks as if the roof is made of cake, and there is icing around the windows.

Hansel This will make a fine lunch. What luck! We'll have a real feast. Come on.

Narrator They ran to the house. Hansel reached up and broke off a bit of the roof.

Hansel Here. Have some of this, Gretel.

Gretel It's sweet! I'm going to taste the window too.

Hansel Wait! I hear something inside the house. Look. The door is opening. Someone is coming out.

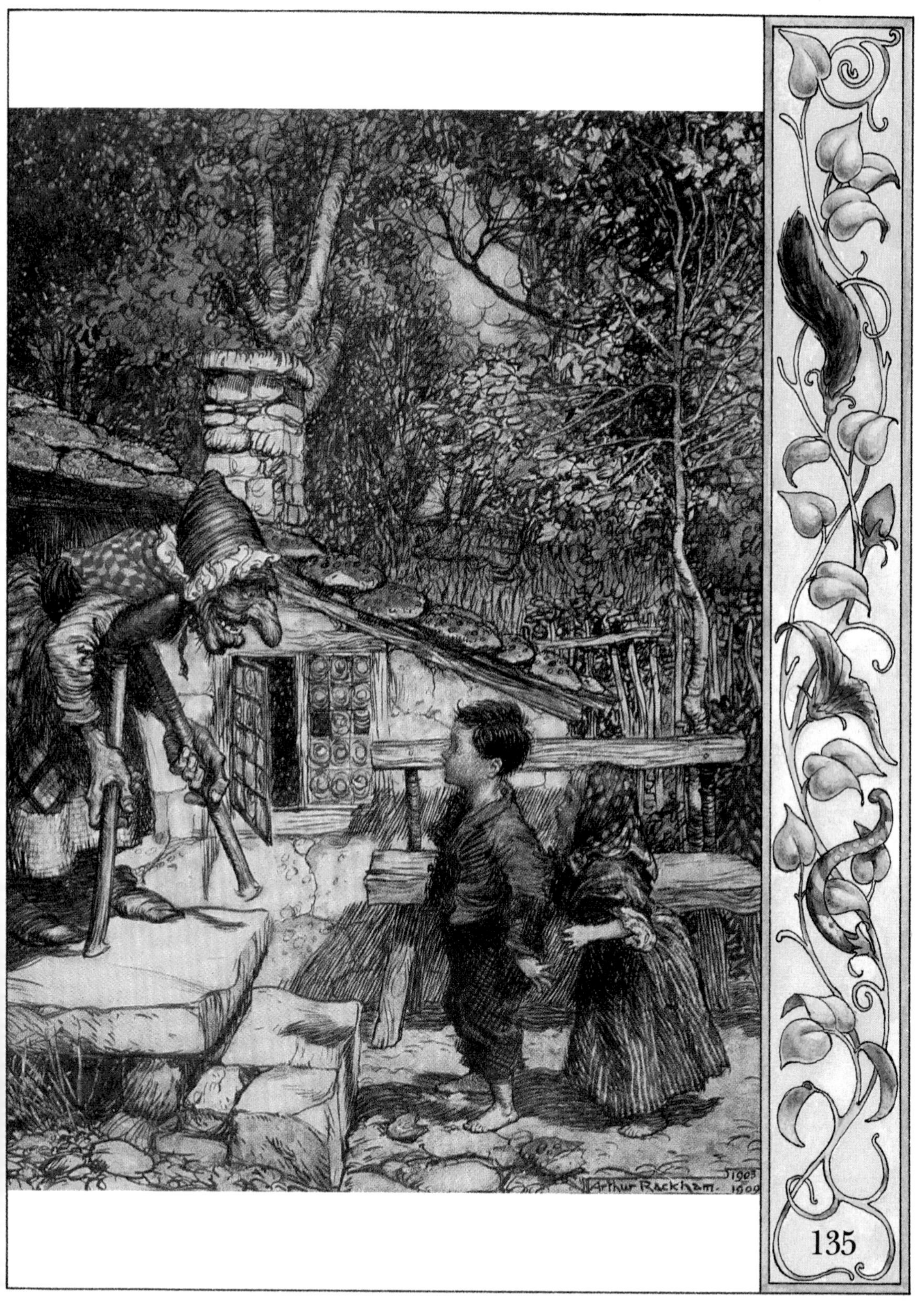
Arthur Rackham
1903
1909

Witch   Nibble, nibble, like a mouse. Who is nibbling at my house?

Narrator   Hansel and Gretel were frightened. They dropped what they had in their hands.

Witch   Ah, my dear children! Come inside. I will give you good things to eat, and I have two little beds where you can sleep. You can stay here with me.

Narrator   So Hansel and Gretel ate well and then went to sleep. They did not know they were in the house of a wicked witch. The witch rubbed her hands as she looked at them, and she laughed a wicked laugh.

Witch   Day after day I wait for children who get lost in the forest. My house of cake is the trap I lay for them. Hansel and Gretel have fallen into my trap. I will cook them and eat them. What a feast I will have!

Hansel   **(waking up)** I had a bad dream. Is it morning already?

Witch   Yes, Hansel. Get up and get to work. See the big cage in that corner? I want you to carry a pile of straw into it.

Hansel   I will do as you say.

Narrator   As soon as Hansel was inside, the witch locked the door of the cage.

Witch   Now I have you!

Hansel   Let me out! Let me out!

Gretel   (**waking up**) Hansel! What is wrong? What is happening?

Witch   What indeed! Get up, my girl. Cook something nice for your brother. He is too thin. He must be fatter. When he is fat enough, I will bake him in my oven. He will be a fine dinner for me.

Gretel   (**crying**) I wish we had been eaten by wild animals in the woods. That would have been better than this.

137

Witch   Stop crying! It won't help you one bit.

Narrator   Each morning the witch would look in on Hansel to see if he was getting fatter.

Witch   Hansel, stretch out your finger, so I can tell if you will soon be fat enough.

Narrator   Hansel would hold out a little bone. The witch, who had weak eyes, could not see what it was. Believing it to be Hansel's finger, she wondered why he was not getting fatter. When four weeks passed and Hansel still seemed so thin, she could wait no longer.

Witch   Now, Gretel. See if the oven is hot. Hansel is still thin, but it is time to kill him and cook him. I won't wait any longer for my feast. Crawl into the oven for me. See if it is hot enough to bake your brother.

Narrator   Gretel felt sure that the witch meant to bake her too. So she held back.

Rackham 1900-1909

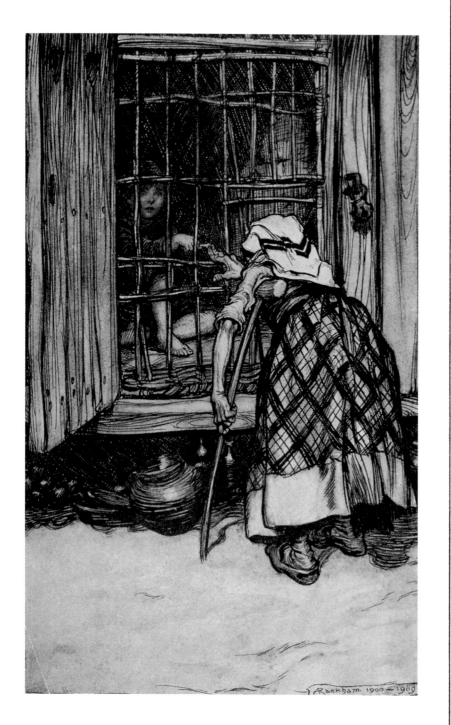

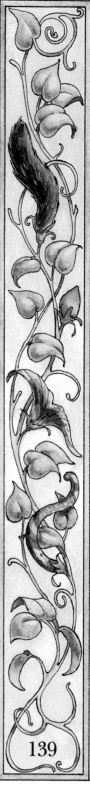

Gretel   I don't know how to open the oven.
How shall I crawl in?

Witch   Silly goose! The opening is big
enough. You just pull this door. Do you see?
I could get in myself.

Gretel   How do you mean? Show me.

Witch   You get in like this.

Narrator   The witch leaned down and put her head in the oven. Quickly Gretel pushed her in and shut the heavy door upon her. Then she left the wicked witch to bake and ran to Hansel. She broke the lock, and he leaped out of the cage.

Gretel   Hansel, we are free!

Hansel   Now, away we go! If only we can find our way out of the witch's forest!

Narrator   Hansel and Gretel soon found a path that led to their house. They rushed into the house and hugged their father. He had not had a happy hour since he left them in the forest, so he was full of joy at the sight of them. After that, they lived together happily. So all was well in the end.

The Gingham Dog and the Calico Cat

by

EUGENE FIELD

The gingham dog and the calico cat
Side by side on the table sat.
'Twas half past twelve, and what do you think!
Not one or the other had slept a wink.

The old Dutch clock and the Chinese plate
Appeared to know, as sure as fate,
There was going to be a terrible fight.
  (I wasn't there. I simply state
  What was told to me by the Chinese plate.)

The gingham dog went, "Bow-wow-wow!"
The calico cat replied, "Mee-ow!"
The air was littered an hour or so
With bits of gingham and calico.

The dog and cat used tooth and claw
In the awfullest way you ever saw.
Oh, how the gingham and calico flew!
　　(Don't think that I exaggerate!
　　I got my news from the Chinese plate.)

Next morning, where the two had sat,
They found no trace of dog or cat.
And some folks think unto this day
That robbers stole the pair away.

But the truth about the cat and pup
Is this: they ate each other up!
Now what do you really think of that!
   (The Chinese plate, it told me so.
   And that is how I came to know.)

The Brocaded Slipper

a Vietnamese Cinderella story by

LYNETTE DYER VUONG

Once there was a man whose wife had died, leaving him with a lovely daughter named Tam. Some time after that, the man married again. His second wife had a daughter of her own. That daughter's name was Cam.

Not many years later, Tam's father died. From that time on, Cam and her mother were mean to Tam. They made her work long hours in the fields and take care of the water buffaloes.

145

One morning the mother called the two girls into the kitchen, and she handed each of them a basket and a pail. "Go down to the pond," she said. "Get these baskets filled by noon. The one who brings home the most fish will have a new red coat."

Tam could hardly believe her ears. A new red coat! She could not remember when she had last had something new. She ran down the road. Cam walked behind.

As soon as they reached the water, Tam set to work, but Cam lay down under a tree.

Tam dipped out pail after pail of water
from the pond. Soon she could see the fish
near the bottom. She stepped into the dirt and
grabbed for them, one by one. When the sun
was high overhead, she had filled her basket
to the top.

Cam came over to her and said, "Oh, Tam,
how dirty you are! You had better wash up
before we go home."

As soon as Tam stepped over to the stream,
Cam filled her own basket with her sister's
fish. Then she ran home.

Tam came back and looked around for Cam, but she was out of sight. Then Tam looked down at her basket. At once she knew what her sister had done. She covered her face with her hands and cried.

All at once, she felt someone touch her head. Looking up, she saw a lovely lady standing by her.

"Why are you crying, my dear?" the lady asked.

Tam pointed to her basket. "My sister took all the fish out of my basket, and I had worked so hard to catch them."

The lady picked up the basket and handed it to Tam.

"Look again," said the lovely lady. "Are you sure there is nothing in your basket?"

Tam looked. To her surprise, she saw one little fish at the bottom.

"This fish will mean more to you than all the ones you lost," said the lady. "Take him home at once, and put him in the well. He will bring you good luck."

Before Tam could thank her, the lady was gone. Tam ran home to do as she had been told.

Each day Tam saved a little of her rice for her fish. She would run out to the well when no one was looking, and she would call:

"Come and eat. Come and eat,
Little fish, pretty fish.
Good rice, fine rice,
From my dish, from my dish."

Then the fish would come up and eat the rice she threw to him. As time went by, the fish grew bigger, and Tam came to love her pet.

But one day her sister Cam was near the well. Tam did not see her. So Cam heard how Tam called the fish and saw her feed him. Cam hurried back to the house to tell her mother.

"Giving good rice to a fish?" said the woman. "We will put an end to that. Let's hope the fish is big enough to make a good lunch for us."

The next day she sent Tam off early with the water buffaloes to find new grass. She handed her a rice cake. "Here is your lunch," she said. "Be sure you get the buffaloes back by sundown."

As soon as Tam was out of sight, Cam took some rice to the well, and she said the words she had heard her sister say. As soon as the fish came up, she grabbed it. Then she took it into the house for her mother to cook for lunch.

That night Tam hurried out to the well with the rice she had saved. She called the fish again and again, but he did not come.

Someone was standing beside her. Looking up, Tam saw the lovely lady who had given her the fish.

"My fish is gone," cried Tam. "Do you know where he is?"

"Cam killed him," said the lady. "But don't cry. He will still bring you good luck. Now you must go and find his bones. When you have found them, divide them into four parts. Put the parts in four jars, and bury the jars, one under each leg of your bed. After one hundred days, dig them up again."

Before Tam could ask anything, the lady was gone. Tam wondered where to start looking for the bones.

Then a rooster came up to her. He said,

"Cock-a-doodle-do, Cock-a-doodle-do.
Give me the rice, and I'll find the bones for you."

Tam threw the rice to him. He ate it quickly.

152

Then he led her to a pile of sticks and leaves.

There were the fish bones, right on top. She picked them up and ran off to find four jars.

That night, Tam started digging. She made four holes in the dirt floor under her bed, one under each leg, and she buried the jars.

Oh, how slowly the time passed as Tam counted off the days she had to wait. At last the hundredth day came. That night, she started digging again. Soon she had all four jars lined up in front of her.

As she opened the first one, Tam gasped. In it was a pair of beautiful red slippers! They were made of brocade. Tiny pictures of birds were stitched into the cloth shoes with golden thread. Tam slipped them on her feet. How good they felt! They fit as if they had been made just for her!

Hurrying back to the other jars, she opened them. From one, she pulled out a beautiful dress. In the others she found lovely gold rings for her fingers and a crown for her head. But she had no place to wear such things, so Tam put them back in the jars. Then she buried them under her bed again.

But Tam could not bear to let the slippers out of her sight. She put them under her covers and lay down to sleep.

The next morning Tam got up before anyone else. She put on her red brocaded slippers and went out to drive the water buffaloes to the river.

But on the way she tripped. One foot slipped into the wet dirt. Oh, her beautiful slipper! The golden threads were black with dirt.

She pulled off the shoe and hurried to a stream close by. There, she washed it. Then she hung up the slipper to dry on the horn of a water buffalo.

All at once the air was filled with the cries of birds. Crows were flying overhead. One of them grabbed Tam's red slipper and flew off with it.

Tam yelled, "Stop! Come back!" She ran after the crow, but it was no use. The crow was soon out of sight. There was no way she could get her beautiful slipper back.

155

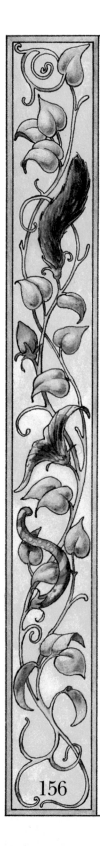

The crow flew on until it came to the palace. The prince was in his garden that morning. As the crow flew overhead, it dropped the red slipper at his feet.

Surprised, the prince picked it up. He turned it over and over in his hands. "This slipper must belong to some beautiful princess," he said. "How I would like to meet her!"

The more he looked at the slipper, the more he wondered about its owner. Soon he could think of nothing else. He told his father, "I know who I want to marry, but I don't know where to find her. I have made up my mind to marry no one but the owner of this slipper."

His father planned a huge feast. He called for all the ladies in his land to come and try on the slipper. The one who could show that her foot fit the slipper would marry the prince.

Cam and her mother heard the news before Tam.

Cam said, "We will go first. You can come after us, Tam. You have to finish your work before you come to the feast. There is a big pile of seeds outside. Pick out all the tiny brown seeds and put them in baskets before you leave the house."

Tam sat down in front of the baskets. What was the use of even trying! There was no way she could finish this job in time to go to the feast.

But then she saw a bird light on one of the baskets, and then another bird flew down. And another! Tam gasped in surprise as she saw the birds doing her work. They were putting all the tiny brown seeds in the baskets, and they were through in no time.

As soon as they flew away, Tam hurried into the house to get dressed. Now she could wear all the beautiful things that were in the jars under her bed. Soon she was ready to go. Tam picked up the slipper that was left and took it with her to the feast.

As she walked in, she saw her sister Cam near the prince. Cam was trying to get her foot into the red brocaded slipper.

"Push harder," Cam's mother was saying to her. "You can get it on your foot if you try."

The prince frowned. "It's clear that it is not her shoe. Take it off. It does not fit. Stop pushing or you will tear the slipper."

Tam came forward.

The prince looked at her, his eyes lighting up. "Will you try on the slipper next?" he asked.

Tam took the slipper in her hand and put it on her foot. Then she pulled out the other slipper.

The prince jumped up as she put her foot in the other slipper.

"I have found the owner of the slipper," he cried. "I have found the one I want to marry."

Not long after, they were married. And all the people in the land were happy for them—except Cam and her mother.

159

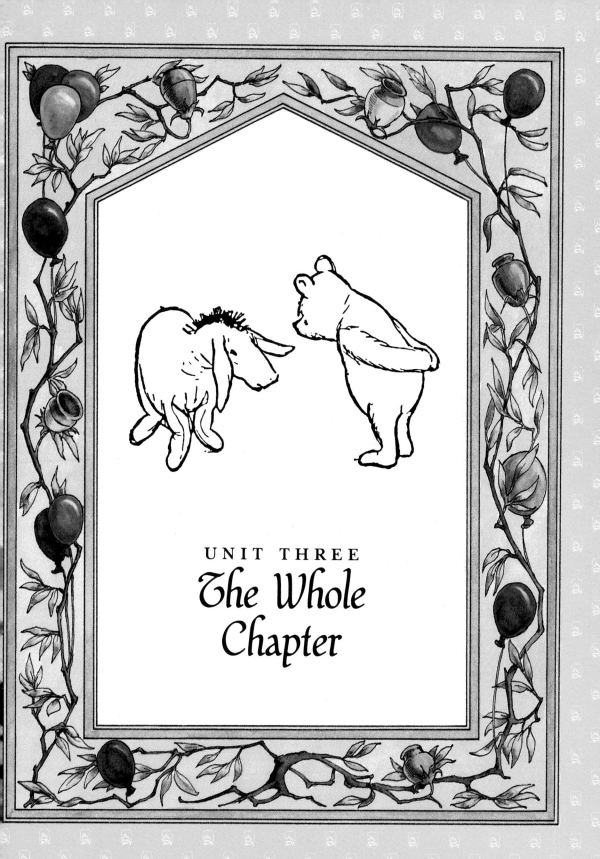

UNIT THREE

The Whole
Chapter

In Which Eeyore Has a Birthday and Gets Two Presents

from

WINNIE-THE-POOH

by

A. A. MILNE

Eeyore, the old grey Donkey, stood by the side of the stream, and looked at himself in the water.

"Pathetic," he said. "That's what it is. Pathetic."

He turned and walked slowly down the stream for twenty yards, splashed across it, and walked slowly back on the other side. Then he looked at himself in the water again.

"As I thought," he said. "No better from *this* side. But nobody minds. Nobody cares. Pathetic, that's what it is."

There was a crackling noise in the bracken behind him, and out came Pooh.

"Good morning, Eeyore," said Pooh.

"Good morning, Pooh Bear," said Eeyore gloomily. "If it *is* a good morning," he said. "Which I doubt," said he.

"Why, what's the matter?"

"Nothing, Pooh Bear, nothing. We can't all, and some of us don't. That's all there is to it."

"Can't all *what?*" said Pooh, rubbing his nose.

"Gaiety. Song-and-dance. Here we go round the mulberry bush."

"Oh!" said Pooh. He thought for a long time, and then asked, "What mulberry bush is that?"

"Bon-hommy," went on Eeyore gloomily. "French word meaning bonhommy," he explained. "I'm not complaining, but There It Is."

Pooh sat down on a large stone, and tried to think this out. It sounded to him like a riddle, and he was never much good at riddles, being a Bear of Very Little Brain. So he sang *Cottleston Pie* instead:

Cottleston, Cottleston, Cottleston Pie,
A fly can't bird, but a bird can fly.
Ask me a riddle and I reply:
"Cottleston, Cottleston, Cottleston Pie."

That was the first verse. When he had finished it, Eeyore didn't actually say that he didn't like it, so Pooh very kindly sang the second verse to him:

Cottleston, Cottleston, Cottleston Pie,
A fish can't whistle and neither can I.
Ask me a riddle and I reply:
"Cottleston, Cottleston, Cottleston Pie."

Eeyore still said nothing at all, so Pooh
hummed the third verse quietly to himself:

Cottleston, Cottleston, Cottleston Pie,
Why does a chicken, I don't know why.
Ask me a riddle and I reply:
"Cottleston, Cottleston, Cottleston Pie."

"That's right," said Eeyore. "Sing. Umty
tiddly, umty-too. Here we go gathering
Nuts and May. Enjoy yourself."
"I am," said Pooh.

"Some can," said Eeyore.
"Why, what's the matter?"
"*Is* anything the matter?"
"You seem so sad, Eeyore."

"Sad? Why should I be sad? It's my birthday. The happiest day of the year."

"Your birthday?" said Pooh in great surprise.

"Of course it is. Can't you see? Look at all the presents I have had." He waved a foot from side to side. "Look at the birthday cake. Candles and pink sugar."

Pooh looked—first to the right and then to the left.

"Presents?" said Pooh. "Birthday cake?" said Pooh. *"Where?"*

"Can't you see them?"

"No," said Pooh.

"Neither can I," said Eeyore. "Joke," he explained. "Ha ha!"

Pooh scratched his head, being a little puzzled by all this.

"But is it really your birthday?" he asked.

"It is."

"Oh! Well, many happy returns of the day, Eeyore."

"And many happy returns to you, Pooh Bear."

"But it isn't *my* birthday."

"No, it's mine."

"But you said 'Many happy returns'—"

"Well, why not? You don't always want to be miserable on my birthday, do you?"

"Oh, I see," said Pooh.

"It's bad enough," said Eeyore, almost breaking down, "being miserable myself, what with no presents and no cake and no candles, and no proper notice taken of me at all, but if everybody else is going to be miserable too—"

This was too much for Pooh. "Stay there!" he called to Eeyore, as he turned and hurried back home as quick as he could; for he felt that he must get poor Eeyore a present of *some* sort at once, and he could always think of a proper one afterwards.

Outside his house he found Piglet, jumping up and down trying to reach the knocker.

"Hallo, Piglet," he said.

"Hallo, Pooh," said Piglet.

"What are *you* trying to do?"

"I was trying to reach the knocker," said Piglet. "I just came round—"

"Let me do it for you," said Pooh kindly. So he reached up and knocked at the door. "I have just seen Eeyore," he began, "and poor Eeyore is in a Very Sad Condition, because it's his birthday, and nobody has taken any notice of it, and he's very Gloomy—you know what Eeyore is—and there he was, and—What a long time whoever lives here is answering this door."

And he knocked again.

"But Pooh," said Piglet, "it's your own house!"

"Oh!" said Pooh. "So it is," he said. "Well, let's go in."

So in they went. The first thing Pooh did was to go to the cupboard to see if he had quite a small jar of honey left; and he had, so he took it down.

"I'm giving this to Eeyore," he explained, "as a present. What are *you* going to give?"

"Couldn't I give it too?" said Piglet. "From both of us?"

"No," said Pooh. "That would *not* be a good plan."

"All right, then, I'll give him a balloon.

I've got one left from my party. I'll go and
get it now, shall I?"

"That, Piglet, is a *very* good idea. It is
just what Eeyore wants to cheer him up.
Nobody can be uncheered with a balloon."

So off Piglet trotted; and in the other
direction went Pooh, with his jar of honey.

It was a warm day, and he had a long way

to go. He hadn't gone more than half-way when
a sort of funny feeling began to creep all
over him. It began at the tip of his nose and
trickled all through him and out at the soles
of his feet. It was just as if somebody inside him
were saying, "Now then, Pooh, time for a little
something."

"Dear, dear," said Pooh, "I didn't know it was as late as that." So he sat down and took the top off his jar of honey. "Lucky I brought this with me," he thought. "Many a bear going out on a warm day like this would never have thought of bringing a little something with him." And he began to eat.

"Now let me see," he thought, as he took his last lick of the inside of the jar, "where was I going? Ah, yes, Eeyore." He got up slowly.

And then, suddenly, he remembered. He had eaten Eeyore's birthday present!

"*Bother!*" said Pooh. "What *shall* I do? I *must* give him *something.*"

For a little while he couldn't think of anything. Then he thought: "Well, it's a very nice pot, even if there's no honey in it, and if I washed it clean, and got somebody to write '*A Happy Birthday*' on it, Eeyore could keep things in it, which might be Useful." So, as he was just passing the Hundred Acre Wood, he went inside to call on Owl, who lived there.

"Good morning, Owl," he said.

"Good morning, Pooh," said Owl.

"Many happy returns of Eeyore's birthday," said Pooh.

"Oh, is that what it is?"

"What are you giving him, Owl?"

"What are *you* giving him, Pooh?"

"I'm giving him a Useful Pot to Keep Things In, and I wanted to ask you—"

"Is this it?" said Owl, taking it out of Pooh's paw.

"Yes, and I wanted to ask you—"

"Somebody has been keeping honey in it," said Owl.

"You can keep *anything* in it," said Pooh earnestly. "It's Very Useful like that. And I wanted to ask you—"

"You ought to write *'A Happy Birthday'* on it."

"*That* was what I wanted to ask you," said Pooh. "Because my spelling is Wobbly. It's good spelling but it Wobbles, and the letters get in the wrong places. Would *you* write *'A Happy Birthday'* on it for me?"

"It's a nice pot," said Owl, looking at it all round. "Couldn't I give it too? From both of us?"

"No," said Pooh. "That would *not* be a good plan. Now I'll just wash it first, and then you can write on it."

Well, he washed the pot out, and dried it, while Owl licked the end of his pencil, and wondered how to spell "birthday."

"Can you read, Pooh?" he asked a little anxiously. "There's a notice about knocking and ringing outside my door, which Christopher Robin wrote. Could you read it?"

"Christopher Robin told me what it said, and *then* I could."

"Well, I'll tell you what *this* says, and then you'll be able to."

So Owl wrote . . . and this is what he wrote:

HIPY PAPY BTHUTHDTH

THUTHDA BTHUTHDY.

Pooh looked on admiringly.

"I'm just saying 'A Happy Birthday'," said Owl carelessly.

"It's a nice long one," said Pooh, very much impressed by it.

"Well, *actually,* of course, I'm saying 'A Very Happy Birthday with love from Pooh.' Naturally it takes a good deal of pencil to say a long thing like that."

"Oh, I see," said Pooh.

While all this was happening, Piglet had gone back to his own house to get Eeyore's balloon. He held it very tightly against himself, so that it shouldn't blow away, and he ran as fast as he could so as to get to Eeyore before Pooh did; for he thought that he would like to be the first one to give a present, just as if he had thought of it without being told by anybody. And running along, and thinking how pleased Eeyore would be, he didn't look where he was going . . .

and suddenly he put his foot in a rabbit hole, and fell down flat on his face.

BANG!!!???***!!!

Piglet lay there, wondering what had happened. At first he thought that the whole world had blown up; and then he thought that perhaps only the Forest part of it had; and then he thought that perhaps only *he* had, and he was now alone in the moon or somewhere, and would never see Christopher Robin or Pooh or Eeyore again. And then he thought, "Well, even if I'm in the moon, I needn't be face downwards all the time," so he got cautiously up and looked about him.

He was still in the Forest!

"Well, that's funny," he thought. "I wonder what that bang was. I couldn't have made such a noise just falling down. And where's my balloon? And what's that small piece of damp rag doing?"

It was the balloon!

"Oh, dear!" said Piglet. "Oh, dear, oh, dearie, dearie, dear! Well, it's too late now. I can't go back, and I haven't another balloon, and perhaps Eeyore doesn't *like* balloons so *very* much."

So he trotted on, rather sadly now, and down he came to the side of the stream where Eeyore was, and called out to him.

"Good morning, Eeyore," shouted Piglet.

"Good morning, Little Piglet," said Eeyore. "If it *is* a good morning," he said. "Which I doubt," said he. "Not that it matters," he said.

"Many happy returns of the day," said Piglet, having now got closer.

Eeyore stopped looking at himself in the stream, and turned to stare at Piglet.

"Just say that again," he said.

"Many hap—"

"Wait a moment."

Balancing on three legs, he began to bring his fourth leg very cautiously up to his ear. "I did this yesterday," he explained, as he fell

down for the third time. "It's quite easy. It's so as I can hear better. . . . There, that's done it! Now then, what were you saying?" He pushed his ear forward with his hoof.

"Many happy returns of the day," said Piglet again.

"Meaning me?"

"Of course, Eeyore."

"My birthday?"

"Yes."

"Me having a real birthday?"

"Yes, Eeyore, and I've brought you a present."

Eeyore took down his right hoof from his right ear, turned round, and with great difficulty put up his left hoof.

"I must have that in the other ear," he said. "Now then."

"A present," said Piglet very loudly.

"Meaning me again?"

"Yes."

"My birthday still?"

"Of course, Eeyore."

"Me going on having a real birthday?"

"Yes, Eeyore, and I brought you a balloon."

"*Balloon?*" said Eeyore. "You did say balloon? One of those big coloured things you blow up? Gaiety, song-and-dance, here we are and there we are?"

"Yes, but I'm afraid—I'm very sorry, Eeyore—but when I was running along to bring it to you, I fell down."

"Dear, dear, how unlucky! You ran too fast, I expect. You didn't hurt yourself, Little Piglet?"

"No, but I—I—oh, Eeyore, I burst the balloon!"

There was a very long silence.

"My balloon?" said Eeyore at last.

Piglet nodded.

"My birthday balloon?"

"Yes, Eeyore," said Piglet sniffing a little. "Here it is. With—with many happy returns of the day." And he gave Eeyore the small piece of damp rag.

"Is this it?" said Eeyore, a little surprised.

Piglet nodded.

"My present?"

Piglet nodded again.

"The balloon?"

"Yes."

"Thank you, Piglet," said Eeyore. "You don't mind my asking," he went on, "but what colour was this balloon when it—when it *was* a balloon?"

"Red."

"I just wondered. . . . Red," he murmured to himself. "My favourite colour. . . . How big was it?"

"About as big as me."

"I just wondered. . . . About as big as Piglet," he said to himself sadly. "My favourite size. Well, well."

Piglet felt very miserable, and didn't know what to say. He was still opening his mouth to begin something, and then deciding that it wasn't any good saying *that*, when he heard a shout from the other side of the river, and there was Pooh.

"Many happy returns of the day," called out Pooh, forgetting that he had said it already.

"Thank you, Pooh, I'm having them," said Eeyore gloomily.

"I've brought you a little present," said Pooh excitedly.

"I've had it," said Eeyore.

Pooh had now splashed across the stream to Eeyore, and Piglet was sitting a little way off, his head in his paws, snuffling to himself.

"It's a Useful Pot," said Pooh. "Here it is. And it's got 'A Very Happy Birthday with love from Pooh' written on it. That's what all that writing is. And it's for putting things in. There!"

When Eeyore saw the pot, he became quite excited.

"Why!" he said. "I believe my Balloon will just go into that Pot!"

"Oh, no, Eeyore," said Pooh. "Balloons are much too big to go into Pots. What you do with a balloon is, you hold the balloon—"

"Not mine," said Eeyore proudly. "Look, Piglet!" And as Piglet looked sorrowfully round, Eeyore picked the balloon up with his teeth, and placed it carefully in the pot; picked it out and put it on the ground; and then picked it up again and put it carefully back.

"So it does!" said Pooh. "It goes in!"

"So it does!" said Piglet. "And it comes out!"

"Doesn't it?" said Eeyore. "It goes in and out like anything."

"I'm very glad," said Pooh happily, "that I thought of giving you a Useful Pot to put things in."

"I'm very glad," said Piglet happily, "that I thought of giving you Something to put in a Useful Pot."

But Eeyore wasn't listening. He was taking
the balloon out, and putting it back again,
as happy as could be. . . .

UNIT FOUR

Numbers, Nature, and Nonsense

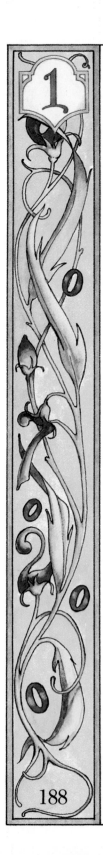

Doctor Dolittle Learns Animal Language

from

THE STORY OF DOCTOR DOLITTLE

by

HUGH LOFTING

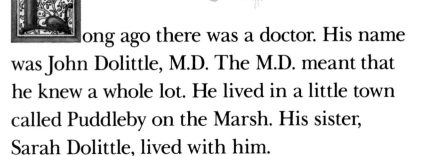

Long ago there was a doctor. His name was John Dolittle, M.D. The M.D. meant that he knew a whole lot. He lived in a little town called Puddleby on the Marsh. His sister, Sarah Dolittle, lived with him.

The Doctor was very fond of animals. He kept many kinds of pets. Besides the goldfish in the pond in his garden, he had rabbits in the kitchen. He also kept white mice in his clothes closet and a porcupine in the living room.

Doctor Dolittle had an old horse too. He kept chickens and sheep and a cow in the backyard. But the pets he liked best were Jip the dog and Polynesia the parrot.

One day an old lady who had a cold came to see Doctor Dolittle. When she went into his waiting room, she sat on the porcupine. After that, she never came to see him any more.

Then his sister, Sarah Dolittle, talked to him. "John," she said. "How can you think that sick people will keep coming here with all these animals in the house?"

"But I like the animals better than the people," said the Doctor.

"You are silly," said his sister. And she walked out of the room.

The parrot Polynesia had been listening.

189

She flew over to the Doctor's table. "Give up being a people's doctor and be an animal doctor," she said.

"Oh, there are lots of animal doctors," said John Dolittle. He put his flower pots outside on the window sill to get some rain.

"Yes," said Polynesia. "But none of them are any good at all. Now listen, Doctor, and I'll tell you something. Did you know that animals can talk?"

"I knew that parrots can talk," said the Doctor.

"Oh, we parrots can talk in two languages," Polynesia said proudly. "People's language and bird language. If I say, 'Polly wants a cracker,' you understand me. But hear this: 'Ka-ka ee-ee fee-fee?' "

"Goodness," cried the Doctor. "What does that mean?"

"That means, 'Is the porridge hot yet?' in bird language."

"My! You don't say so!" said the Doctor. "Tell me some more." He rushed over to the desk and came back with paper and pencil. "Now don't go too fast. I want to write it down. Give me the birds' ABC first, slowly now."

So that was the way the Doctor came to know that animals had a language of their own and could talk to one another. All that afternoon, while it was raining, Polynesia gave him bird words to put down on paper.

When the dog Jip came over to them, the parrot said to the Doctor, "See, he's talking to you."

"Looks to me as though he were lifting his ear," said the Doctor.

But animals don't always speak with their mouths," said the parrot.

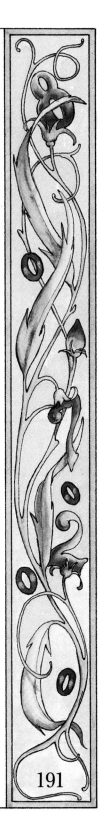

"They talk with their ears, with their feet, with their tails—with everything. Do you see now the way he's turning up one side of his nose?"

"What's that mean?" asked the Doctor.

"That means, 'Can't you see that it has stopped raining?' " said Polynesia. "He is asking you a question. Dogs nearly always use their noses for asking questions."

After a while, with the parrot's help, the Doctor got to learn the language of the animals so well that he could talk to them himself. And he could understand what they said to him.

Then he gave up being a people's doctor for good. He became an animal doctor, and a very fine one.

One day a plow horse was brought to him. The poor thing was as glad as could be to find a man who could talk in horse language.

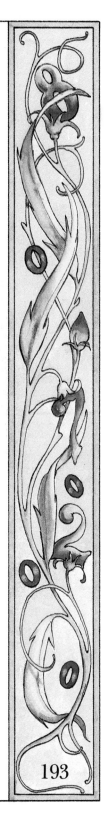

"You know," said the horse. "That doctor over the hill knows nothing at all. He saw that my eyes were red and watery. So he has been treating me for six weeks—for a cold. But I don't have a cold. My eyes are red and watery because I need glasses."

The horse tossed his head and went on, "I don't see why horses shouldn't wear glasses, the same as people. But that silly man never even thought of glasses. I tried to tell him. What I need is a pair of glasses."

"Of course. Of course," said the Doctor. "I'll get you some as soon as I can test your eyes."

"I would like a pair like yours," said the horse. "Only green. They'll keep the sun out of my eyes while I'm plowing the field."

"Fine," said Doctor Dolittle. "Green ones are what you shall have." By the next week, he had a fine big pair of green glasses ready.

Then the Doctor put them on the plow horse. The horse could see as well as ever.

Soon many farm animals could be seen wearing glasses in the country around Puddleby on the Marsh.

Now all these animals told their friends that there was a doctor in Puddleby who could talk their language. The word traveled quickly.

So the Doctor's big garden was always full of animals trying to get in to see him.

Doctor Dolittle became well known among the animals far and near. He was happy and liked his life very much.

• • • • •

That is how Doctor Dolittle started talking with the animals. He kept talking with them in the series of Doctor Dolittle books by Hugh Lofting. You can find the books in the library.

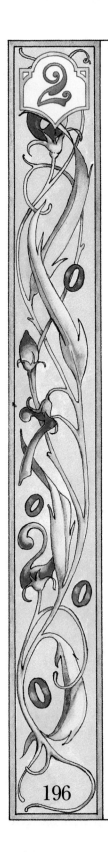

The Chimp Who Learned Language

from

THE STORY OF NIM

by

ANNA MICHEL

You have read that Doctor Dolittle talked with animals. But you know that he was a make-believe person. His story did not really happen.

Now you are going to read a true story. The story is about real people who talked with a real animal. It is the story of Nim, a chimp who learned language.

On November 21, 1973, a baby chimp was born. He was named Nim. At that time, Nim seemed just like any other baby chimp. But he became very special. He became one of the first chimps who could really "talk" to people.

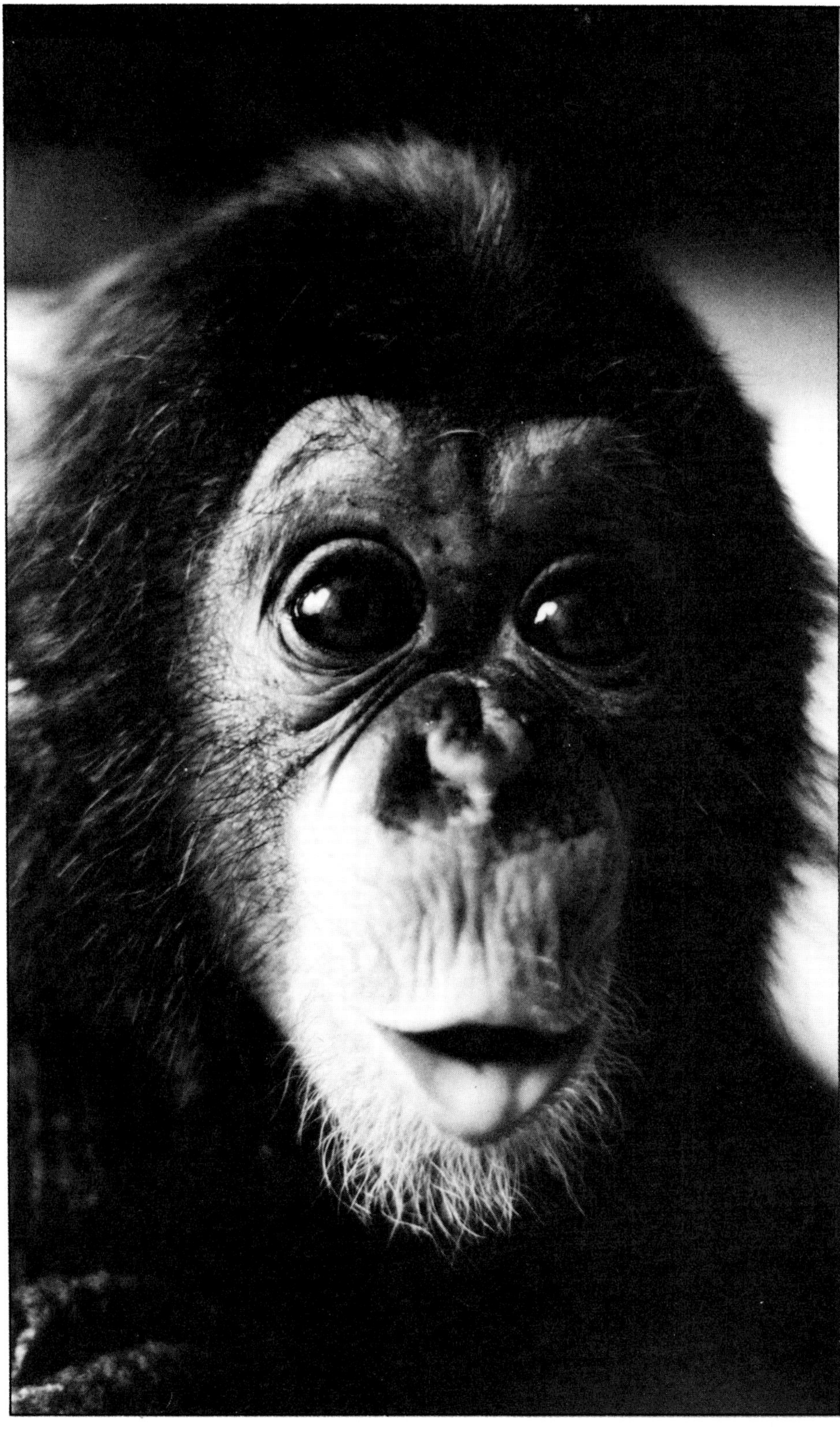

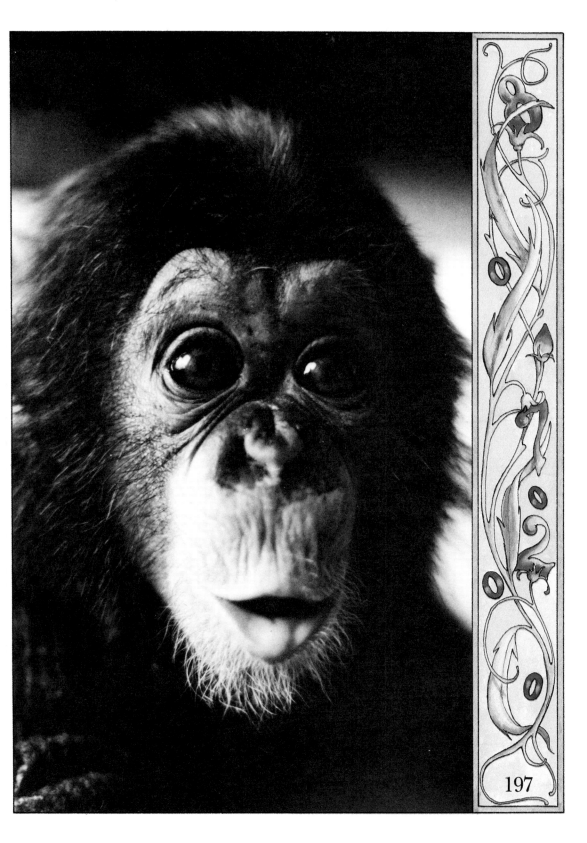

Of course, he could not make the sounds that people make when they speak. But he was taught to "talk" with his hands— the way some deaf people do. For four years many people worked with him to help him learn to talk.

As a baby, he was placed with the LaFarge family. From his first day with the LaFarges, Nim was "talked" to in American Sign Language, the language of the deaf.

Nim loved his family. He watched the signs they made as they talked to him. And slowly, in the way a baby begins to understand words, Nim began to understand signs.

When Mrs. LaFarge brought Nim his bottle, she would touch her thumb to her mouth, making the sign for *drink*. Then she would shape Nim's hands to make the *drink* sign.

One day, when Nim was two and a half months old, Mrs. LaFarge held up his bottle.

Nim put his thumb to his mouth and signed *drink*. This was the first time Nim had made a sign all by himself.

He learned more signs quickly. Soon Nim was making signs for *up, sweet, give, eat,* and *more.*

Then he started "school." Nim's school was a special classroom, just for him. There, his teachers could "talk" with him all day.

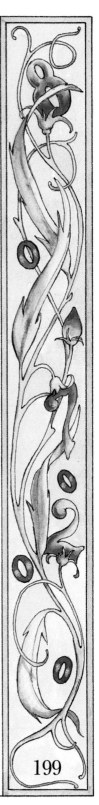

Nim and his teachers talked about everything they did. The teachers made notes of his signs. When he had used a sign for five days, and three different teachers had seen the sign, it was counted as a word he knew.

Nim was taught to do for himself. He had to learn to brush his teeth, dress himself, and clean up after he ate.

Each morning he would sign *toothbrush* happily. Nim never minded brushing his teeth. He loved the taste of the toothpaste.

Next came hand washing. First Nim washed his hands. Then he washed his feet. When he was finished, he asked for hand cream.

Now it was time to get dressed. He had to sign *shirt* before putting on his shirt. Then it was time for Nim to eat. He loved banana pancakes.

After eating, Nim wanted to wash the dishes. *Give,* he signed to get the dishcloth.

He turned on the water, signing *water.* Then he rubbed the dishes until they were all clean.

As Nim learned more words, he started to put signs together. He would say *me hat* or *give hat* if he wanted the hat his teacher was holding.

If Nim wanted to play, he would sign *play me Nim* and *tickle me more.* Like a young child, Nim could understand much more than he could say.

Nim learned that he could name things and get what he needed. But he could also use language to fool people. His teachers would stop what they were doing whenever Nim would sign *bathroom.* So, sometimes Nim would sign *bathroom* just to get out of a lesson.

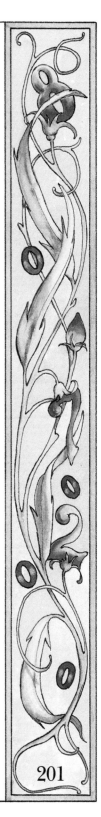

Sometimes he signed *sleep,* even though he wasn't tired. But his teachers learned to spot when Nim was not telling them the truth. He wouldn't look them in the eye when he made those signs.

By the time he was almost four years old, Nim had learned to use signs for 125 words. His teachers then started to work with other animals. Nim went to live on an island with other chimps who also knew sign language.

• • • •

For many years people wished they could talk with animals. But they thought that only make-believe people like Doctor Dolittle talked with animals. They thought that, in real life, it couldn't be done.

But the people who worked with Nim tried to do what "couldn't be done"—and they did it.

It Couldn't Be Done

by

EDGAR A. GUEST

Somebody said that it couldn't be done.
But he with a chuckle replied
That "maybe it couldn't," but he would be one
Who wouldn't say so till he'd tried.

So he buckled right in with a trace of a grin
On his face. If he worried, he hid it.
He started to sing as he tackled the thing
That couldn't be done, and he did it.

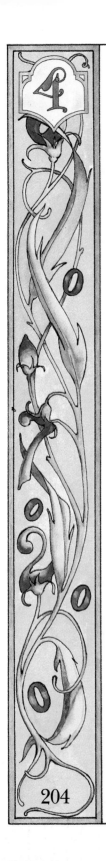

How the Puppet's Nose Grows

from

THE ADVENTURES OF PINOCCHIO

by

CARLO COLLODI

This best-known part of the book tells what happens when the wooden puppet Pinocchio lies.

Pinocchio's friend, the Blue Fairy, was good to him. She helped him and pushed him and questioned him the way a good mother would. She knew that Pinocchio had a lot to learn before he could turn from a wooden puppet into a real boy.

"Where are the gold pieces that you were told to take to your father?" she asked Pinocchio.

"I lost them," said the puppet. But he told a lie. He had them in his pocket.

As he spoke, his wooden nose became two inches longer.

"And where did you lose them?" she asked.

"In the woods nearby," said Pinocchio.

At this second lie, his nose grew a few more inches.

"Then we'll look for them in the woods nearby," said the Blue Fairy. "Things that are lost there are always found."

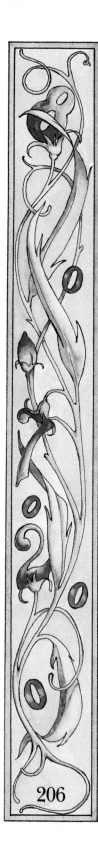

"Wait!" said the puppet. "Now I remember. I did not lose the gold pieces in the woods. I dropped them when I was running across a field."

At this third lie, his nose became longer than ever. It was so long that he could not even turn around. If he turned to the right, he knocked it against the wall. If he turned to the left, he hit the door. If he raised it a bit, he almost put the Blue Fairy's eyes out.

She sat looking at him and laughing.

"Why do you laugh?" the puppet asked her. He was worried at the sight of his nose.

"I am laughing at your lies," she said.

"How do you know I am lying?" asked Pinocchio.

"Lies, my boy, are easy to spot. They are known in a second. When a wooden puppet tells a lie, his nose grows."

Pinocchio tried to run out of the room.

But his nose had become so long that he could not get it through the door. He was so frightened that he was ready to cry. "What am I to do?" said Pinocchio. "Will I never get outdoors again?"

The Blue Fairy felt sorry for him. She snapped her fingers and some woodpeckers flew in and landed on Pinocchio's nose.

They pecked and pecked at that wooden nose. Soon it was as small as it had been before Pinocchio told his lies.

•   •   •   •

The puppet Pinocchio gets in and out of trouble many times in Carlo Collodi's book *The Adventures of Pinocchio.*

Maybe you would like to read the book and see the movie about Pinocchio.

Broom Hilda and Pinocchio

by

RUSSELL MYERS

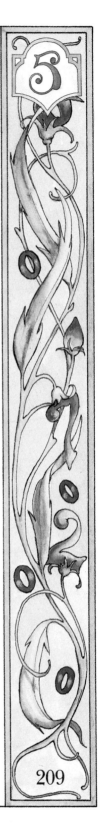

Goops

by

GELETT BURGESS

The Goops they lick their fingers,
And the Goops they lick their knives.
They spill the broth on the tablecloth.
They lead disgusting lives!

The Goops they talk while eating,
And loud and fast they chew.
And that is why I'm glad that I
Am not a Goop—are you?

210

The Vulture

by

HILAIRE BELLOC

The vulture eats between his meals,
And that's the reason why
He very, very rarely feels
As well as you and I.

His eye is dull, his head is bald,
His neck is growing thinner.
Oh! What a lesson for us all
To only eat at dinner!

The Donkey and the Grasshoppers

from

AESOP'S FABLES

There was once a donkey who heard some grasshoppers singing. "How sweet their voices are," he thought. The donkey wished his voice were as soft and sweet as theirs. He was tired of being laughed at for his loud "Hee-haw."

So he asked them, "What makes your voices sound so sweet? Do you eat some special food?"

"Just dew," they told him. "We live on the fresh dew that is on the grass each morning. It is food and drink enough for us. Maybe it gives us sweet voices."

"Then it will do the same for me," said the donkey.

The next day he ate nothing but the fresh wet dew that had settled on the tall grass. "If I eat like the grasshoppers, then I will have a voice like theirs," thought the donkey.

But his voice did not become soft and sweet. There was still no music in his "Hee-haw." He just became weak and thin from going hungry, and his voice was still laughed at— even by the grasshoppers, now.

What works for others may not work for you.

The Crocodile

by

LAURA RICHARDS

Why does the crocodile weep, Mamma?
　　Why does the crocodile weep?
He has a sorrow, dear my child.
It makes him sad; it makes him wild.
　　He cannot be a sheep!

He cannot wag a woolly tail,
　　He cannot say, "Ba! ba!"
He cannot jump, nor flimp nor flump,
　　Nor gallop off afar.

Be sorry for the crocodile,
　　But don't go very near.
Howe'er he bawl, whate'er befall,
　　Don't try to dry his tear!

The Dragon and the Red Cross Knight

from

THE FAERIE QUEENE

by

EDMUND SPENSER

ong ago there lived a wise and good queen. Each year she held a twelve-day feast for her people, and they could ask her for favors. She would grant as many as she could.

One year at the feast, a young man came to the queen. "Someone at this feast may ask for the help of a brave knight," he said. "If that happens, please choose me."

215

"I wish to fight evil," he said.

The queen looked at the young man. He had no sword or shield, but he had a wish to serve. "We shall see," said the queen.

The young man waited. Day after day he stayed by the queen, but the call for a knight did not come.

On the last day of the feast a fair lady came into town, riding on a white horse. Her name was Lady Una. She came before the queen with tears in her eyes.

"Good Queen," she said. "An evil dragon killed my brother. I have come to you, bearing my brother's sword and shield. Please grant me the help of one of your knights. Have you one who is not afraid to fight an evil dragon?"

"Lady Una," said the queen, "I can grant you that favor. Leave your brother's sword and shield with me. Return in an hour, and your knight will be ready to ride with you."

The young man had jumped up.

The queen turned to him and pointed to the shield Lady Una had left. "See the cross of red on that shield. The knight who bears the red cross must be brave and good. I send you forth as the Red Cross Knight."

The next day Lady Una and the Red Cross Knight rode forth. They went through the woods to the hills. Then they rode over the hills to the cave of the evil dragon.

There, they came upon the dragon. She was huge with sharp claws and wild eyes and a long tail that she lashed about. Her eyes were as red as fire.

Lady Una drew back. "Sir Knight, take care," she said.

The Red Cross Knight quickly raised his spear and rode toward the dragon.

As soon as the dragon saw him, she was up and she came at him.

Just as the knight was close enough for a mighty strike, the dragon lashed at him with her tail.

The blow knocked him off his horse.

As he got to his feet, the dragon coiled her tail around his legs.

The Red Cross Knight gripped the dragon's neck. So strong was his grip that it made her fall back. The knight got his legs free from her coiled tail, and he pulled away.

The dragon lashed her tail, but the knight jumped aside. He grabbed his sword and with one blow, he cut off her head.

"Well done, Sir Knight!" cried Lady Una. "May all your fights with evil dragons end this way."

They took the head of the dragon back to the queen, and many times thereafter, the queen sent forth the Red Cross Knight to fight evil.

A Riddle

by

CHRISTINA ROSSETTI

There is one that has a head without an eye.
And there's one that has an eye without a head.
You may find the answers if you try.
And when all is said,
Half the answer hangs upon a thread.

As I Was Going to St. Ives

from

MOTHER GOOSE

As I was going to St. Ives,
I met a man with seven wives.
Each wife had seven sacks.
Each sack had seven cats.
Each cat had seven kits.
Kits, cats, sacks, and wives,
How many were going to St. Ives?

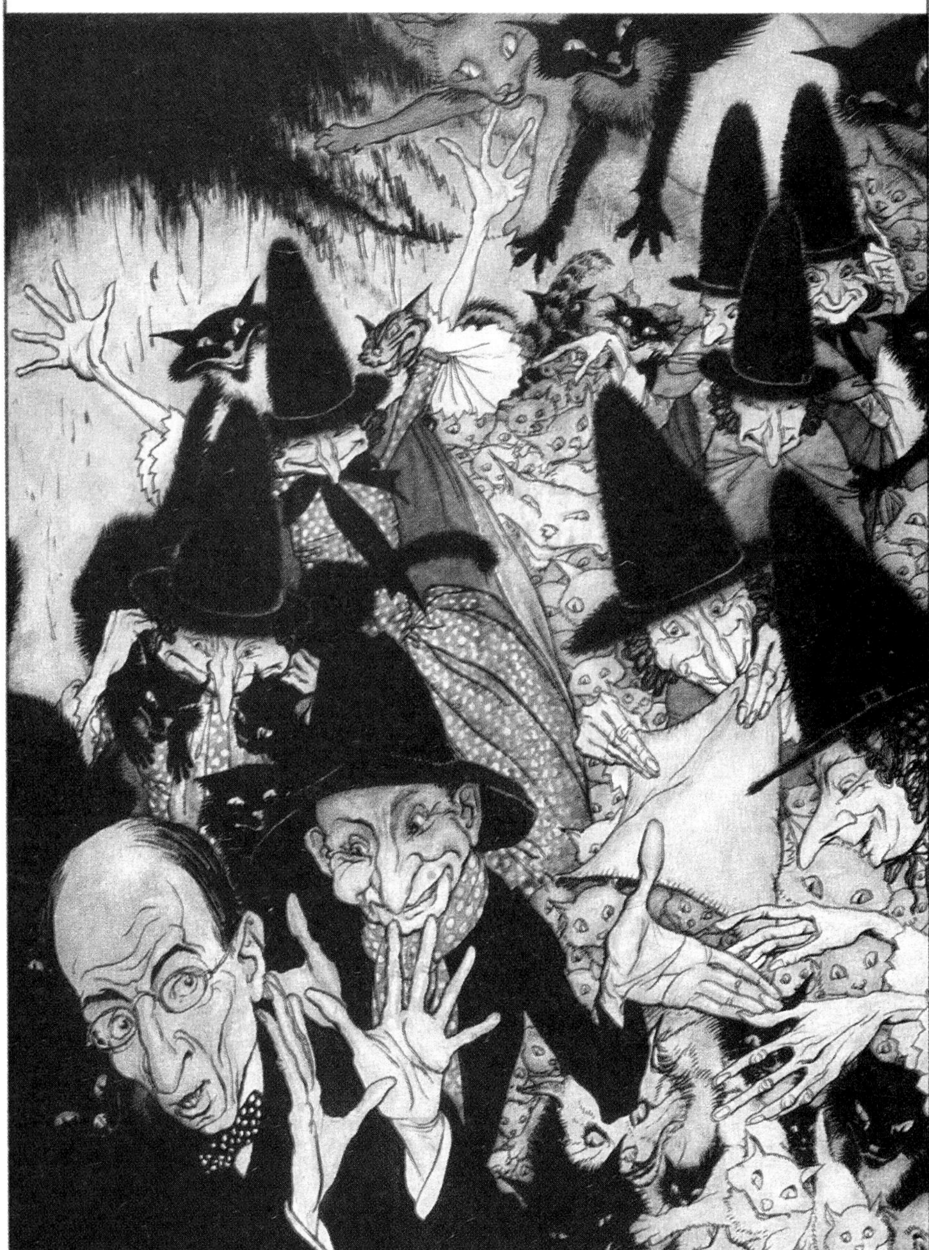
ARTHUR RACKHAM 1912

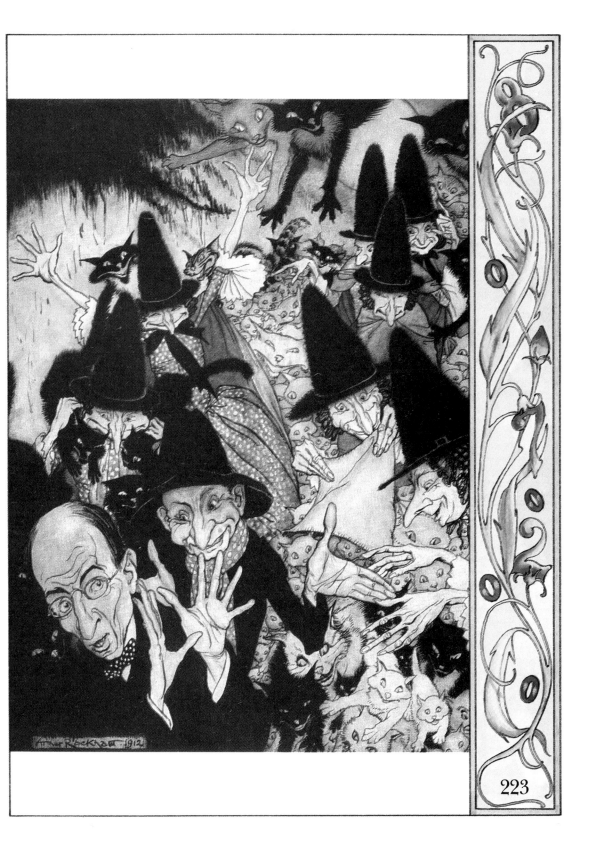

Rapunzel

by the

BROTHERS GRIMM

Once upon a time there lived a man and wife who had long wished for a child. From a window in their house they could see a beautiful garden on the hillside. But no one went into that garden because it belonged to a witch. Everyone was afraid of her.

One day the wife looked out the window. In the garden she saw the finest lettuce she had ever set eyes on. It was so green and so good that she began to wish for some. The more she looked, the more she longed for it.

This went on for days. Since she knew she could not have any lettuce from the witch's garden, she grew more and more unhappy. She lost her color and looked sick.

Then the man was worried. He asked, "What is the matter, dear wife?"

"Oh," said she, "I shall die if I can't have some of the lettuce from the witch's garden."

The man thought to himself, "I could not bear to lose my wife. I will get her some of that lettuce, no matter what happens."

So, in the evening, he tiptoed over the path to the witch's garden. Quickly he picked a head of lettuce, but before he could get away, the witch caught hold of him.

"Robber!" she cried. "Why do you come by night to take my lettuce?"

"Oh, please," the man said. "It is for my wife. She has so great a longing for it that she will die if she does not have some to eat."

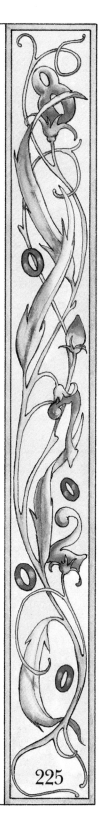

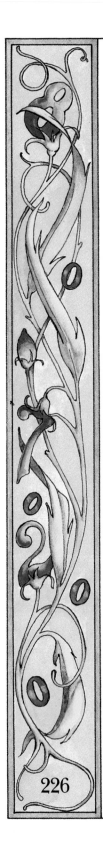

The witch frowned. "If it is as you say, you may have the lettuce this one time. But you must give me the child your wife will bear. I will care for it like a mother."

The man did not know what else he could do, so he said she could have the child. When the child was born, the witch took her away. She gave the child the name Rapunzel.

Rapunzel was a beautiful child. She had long, long hair that was never cut. When she was twelve years old, the witch shut her up in a tower in the woods. It had no steps and no door, and it had only one small window near the top of the tower.

When the witch wished to be let in, she stood below and called, "Rapunzel, Rapunzel! Let down your long hair."

When Rapunzel heard the witch call, she opened the window and let down her hair. The witch would take hold of it and climb up.

One day the prince was walking through the woods. He came to the tower, and he heard a voice singing so sweetly that he stood still and listened.

It was Rapunzel trying to pass the time by singing.

The prince wished to get to her, but he saw that there was no door to the tower. He walked away. But her singing stayed with him, and he kept going back into the woods to listen to her.

Once, when he was nearby, he saw the witch come up. He listened while she called out, "Rapunzel, Rapunzel! Let down your long hair." Then he watched while the witch climbed up.

"Ah," he said to himself. "Since that is the ladder, I will climb it."

The next day, he went to the tower and cried, "Rapunzel, Rapunzel! Let down your long hair."

She let down her hair, and the prince climbed up it.

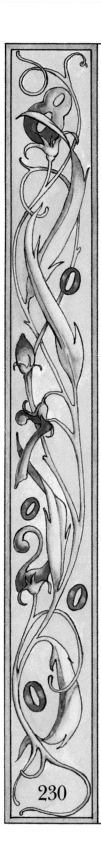

Rapunzel was frightened when she saw the prince, for she had never seen a man before. But he told her that he had fallen in love with her, just by listening to her sing. He visited her again and again, so she soon got over her fear.

"He is young and kind," Rapunzel thought to herself. "I like him much better than the witch who keeps me here."

One day the prince asked her to be his wife.

"I would be happy to leave this tower and go with you," she said. "But I do not know how I shall get out."

"When next I come to you, I will bring some rope," said the prince. "We will make a ladder. You can get down on it, and I will take you away with me."

While she waited for him, the witch came to see Rapunzel. The witch knew nothing about the prince.

Without thinking, Rapunzel said to her, "How is it that you climb up here so slowly? The prince is with me in a minute."

"What is this I hear?" cried the witch. "I thought I had hidden you away where no one could get to you. But no! You have been keeping things from me."

She grabbed Rapunzel by her beautiful hair and hit the girl hard with her hand. Then she started cutting, and soon all of Rapunzel's long hair was on the floor.

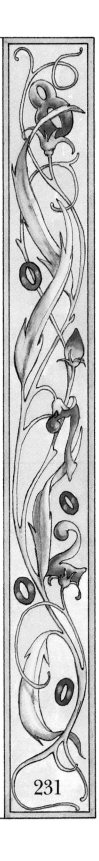

The witch was still so angry that she used her magic to put Rapunzel in a faraway place where she lived in great sadness.

That evening, the prince came and cried, "Rapunzel, Rapunzel! Let down your long hair."

The witch let the hair down, and the prince climbed up. But instead of his dear Rapunzel, he found the witch looking at him with angry eyes.

"You came for your dear Rapunzel," cried the witch. "But the sweet bird sits no longer in this nest."

"No!" cried the prince.

"Rapunzel is lost to you," said the witch. "You will see her no more."

The prince was beside himself with sadness. He jumped from the tower, and the thorns on which he fell put out his eyes. Then he wandered through the woods, calling for his Rapunzel.

After wandering for a long time, he came to the faraway place where the witch had put Rapunzel. There he heard a voice that he thought he knew. When he reached the place it seemed to come from, Rapunzel saw him. She put her arms around him, and she cried.

As her tears touched his eyes, they became clear again, and he could see with them as well as ever.

Then they went together to his castle where they lived long and happily.

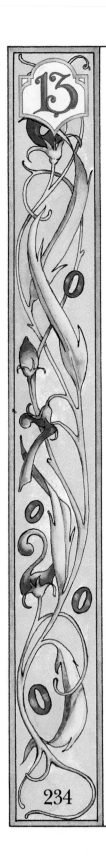

A Swing Song

by

WILLIAM ALLINGHAM

Swing, swing.
Sing, sing.
Here's my throne and I am king!
Swing, sing.
Swing, sing.
Farewell, Earth. I'm on the wing!

Low, high.
Here I fly,
Like a bird through sunny sky.
Free, free,
Over the lea,
Over the mountain, over the sea.

No, no.
Low, low.
Sweeping daisies with my toe.
Slow, slow.
To and fro,
Slow—slow—slow—slow.

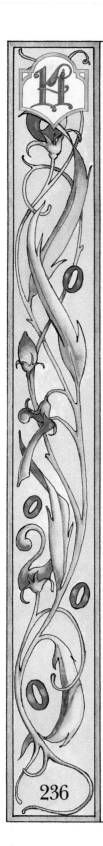

Flying with Peter Pan

from

PETER PAN

by

J. M. BARRIE

Each night Mrs. Darling went upstairs, read a story to her three children, and then put them to bed. Wendy was the oldest of the Darling children, then John, then little Michael. They had a dog named Nana. They were much like all the other families on their street—until one magic night.

That night Mrs. Darling sat in the rocking chair, singing to her children until they slipped into the land of sleep. Then she nodded off too.

But she woke up with a start when the window blew open. A boy leaped in— or did he fly in? Mrs. Darling was not sure.

He was a lovely boy, about the size of her daughter Wendy. His hair was windblown. He was dressed in leaves, and he looked cocky and pleased with himself.

Mrs. Darling started up with a little cry, and as if in answer to a bell, the dog Nana trotted into the room. The dog jumped at the boy, but he leaped lightly out the window.

Again Mrs. Darling cried out, this time in fear for the boy. She thought he would be hurt, falling one story down to the street. Mrs. Darling ran downstairs and out the door to look for his little body, but it was not there. She looked up, and in the dark night she saw what she thought was a shooting star.

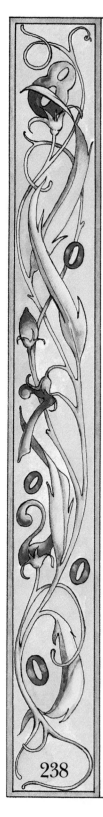

Mrs. Darling went back upstairs and found the dog with something in her mouth. It was the boy's shadow. Nana had snapped at the boy as he leaped out the window. She was not fast enough to catch him. But his shadow had not had time to get out with him, and the dog caught it.

Mrs. Darling held up the shadow and looked at it carefully. There was nothing special about it, so she gave it back to the dog Nana.

Nana put it out the window. She barked, meaning, "He is sure to come back for it. Let's leave it hanging here where he can get it easily."

But Mrs. Darling could not leave it hanging out the window. It looked so much like the washing. So she folded it up and put it in a drawer.

A few nights later Mr. and Mrs. Darling
went out for dinner. That night, as soon as
the Darling children were asleep, the window
blew open again. In flew the same boy,
looking for his shadow.

He hunted all over the room, in the corners,
under the beds. He threw clothes on the floor.
He opened drawer after drawer. Then he
found it. His shadow! He danced around
the room.

He had thought that when he and
his shadow were brought near each other,
they would join like drops of water. But they
did not. So he tried to stick his shadow
to his feet with soap. This did not work.
Then he sat down on the floor and cried.

His crying woke Wendy, and she sat up in bed. She was not frightened at seeing a stranger sitting on the floor, crying. She was just interested.

"Boy," she said softly. "My name is Wendy Moira Angela Darling. What is your name?"

"Peter Pan," he said.

"Is that all?"

"Yes," he said, a bit sharply. For the first time in his life, he felt that maybe it was too short a name.

Wendy asked where he lived.

"Second to the right," said Peter. "And then straight on till morning."

"What a funny address."

Peter had a sinking feeling. For the first time he felt that maybe it was a funny address.

"No, it isn't," he said.

"I mean," Wendy said nicely, "is that what they put on letters?"

"I don't get any letters," he said.

"But doesn't your mother get letters?" Wendy asked.

"Don't have a mother."

"Oh, Peter," said Wendy. "No wonder you were crying." She got out of bed and ran to him.

"I wasn't crying about mothers," he said. "I was crying because I can't get my shadow to stick on. Besides, I wasn't crying."

"Your shadow has come off?"

"Yes," said Peter.

Then Wendy saw the shadow on the floor, and she was so sorry for Peter. But she could not help smiling when she saw he had been trying to stick it on with soap.

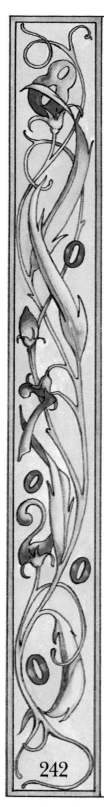

Wendy knew at once what to do. "I'll sew it on for you," she said. "But it will hurt a little."

"Oh, I won't cry," said Peter, who was already feeling that he had never cried in his life. And he did not cry. When Wendy finished, his shadow was back with him.

Soon Peter was jumping around in the wildest joy. He had already forgotten about Wendy's help. He leaped around the room as if he had stuck the shadow on himself.

"How clever I am!" he crowed.

Wendy tapped her foot. "Of course, I did nothing," she said.

"You did a little," Peter said, and he kept dancing around.

"A little!" she replied. "If I am of no use, I shall go back to bed." She pulled the covers up over her face.

"Wendy," said Peter. "Please come out and tell me a story. I've been flying to your window at night to hear the stories your mother reads. I live with the lost children in Never Never Land, and none of us know any stories. Your mother was telling such a lovely story."

"Which story was it?" asked Wendy.

"The one about the prince who couldn't find the lady who lost the glass slipper."

"Oh, Peter," said Wendy. "That was Cinderella. He found her, and they lived happily ever after."

243

Peter was so glad that he rose from the floor and hurried to the window.

"Where are you going?" asked Wendy.

"I'm going to fly back and tell the other children in Never Never Land," he said. "They all want to know how that story ended."

"Don't go, Peter," said Wendy. "I know lots of stories that I could tell you."

Peter came back. But he took Wendy's hand and started drawing her toward the window.

"Let me go," she said. But she didn't pull away.

"Wendy," said Peter. "Do fly to Never Never Land with me. You can tell stories to all the lost children."

Of course Wendy was very pleased to be asked. But she said, "Oh, dear, I can't. Think how much my mother would miss me, Peter. Besides, I can't fly."

"I'll teach you," said Peter.

"Oh, how lovely to fly!" cried Wendy.

"I'll teach you to jump on the wind's back," Peter went on. "Then away we'll go. Wendy, Wendy, when you are sleeping in your silly bed, you might be flying about with me, saying funny things to the stars."

"Peter, would you teach my brothers John and Michael to fly too?"

"If you like," he said.

Wendy ran to John and Michael and shook them. "Wake up!" she cried. "Peter Pan is here, and he will teach us to fly."

John rubbed his eyes. "Then I shall get up."

Michael was up by this time too. He looked at Peter. "Can you really fly?" he asked.

Instead of troubling to answer him, Peter flew around the room.

It looked easy. They tried it first from their floor and then from the beds, but they always went down instead of up.

"How do you do it, Peter?" asked John, rubbing his knee.

"You just think lovely thoughts, and they lift you up in the air," said Peter. He showed them again. "Now just move your arms like this, and then let go."

They were all on their beds. Michael let go first. He did not quite mean to let go, but he did it, and at once he was floating across the room.

"I'm flying!" he screamed.

John let go. He passed Wendy near the top of the door.

"Oh, lovely!" cried Wendy.

"Look at me!" John shouted, flapping his arms.

Up and down they went, and round and round.

John flew to the window. "Why shouldn't we all fly outside?"

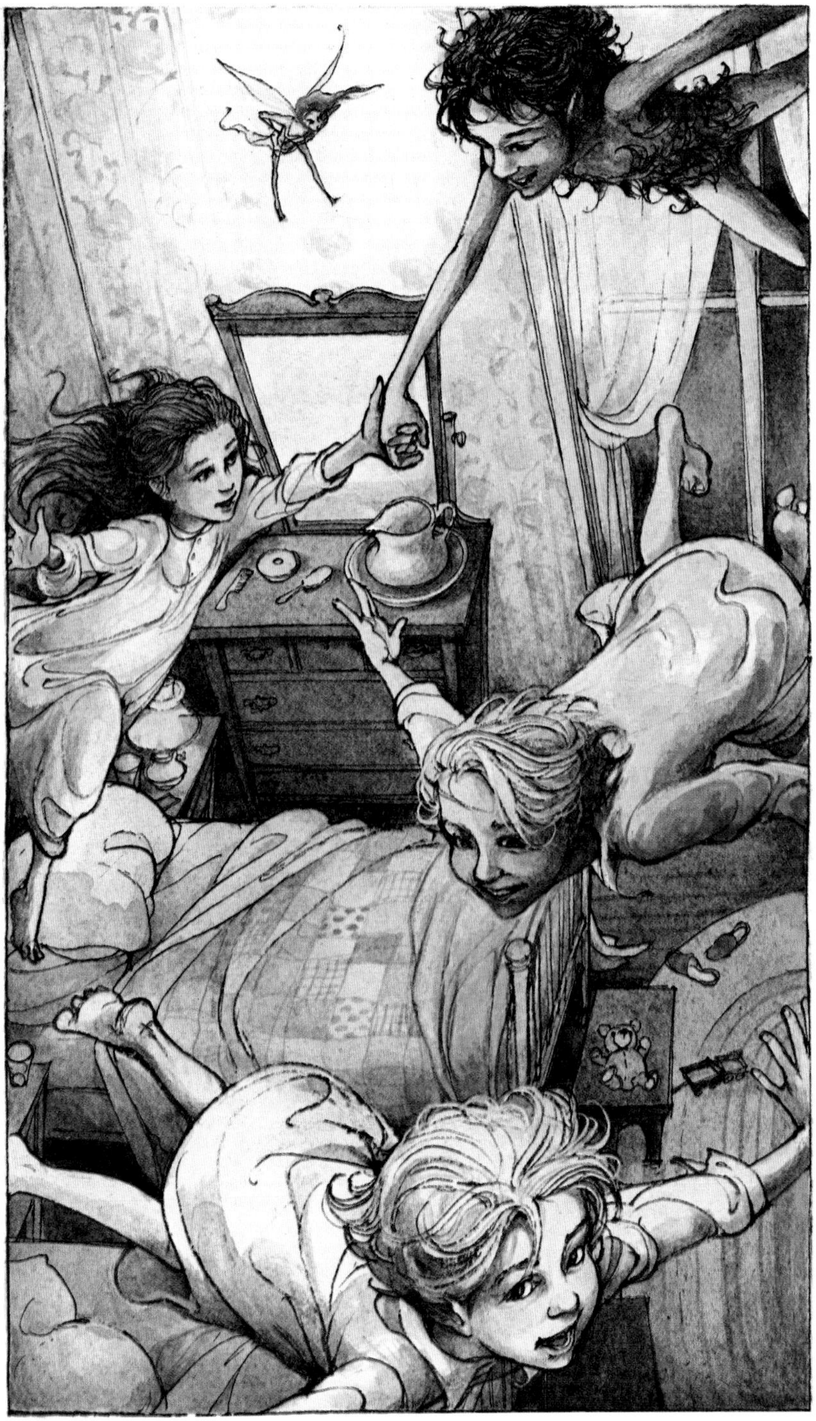

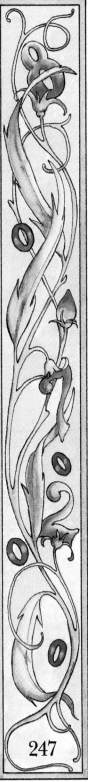

Of course, it was to this that Peter had been leading them.

Michael was ready, but Wendy was hanging back.

"Come with me," said Peter. "We'll touch the stars."

"Oh," cried Wendy. "To touch a star!" And she was at the window.

"Follow me," called Peter as he flew out into the night. And Wendy and John and Michael were right behind him, on their way to Never Never Land.

.   .   .   .

You can find out what happened in Never Never Land if you read the book *Peter Pan.* So many people have loved the story that it has been made into a play, a musical, and a movie.

My Shadow

by

ROBERT LOUIS STEVENSON

I have a little shadow that goes
    in and out with me,
And what can be the use of him
    is more than I can see.
He is very, very like me from the heels
    up to the head.
And I see him jump before me when I jump
    into my bed.

The funniest thing about him is the way
    he likes to grow—
Not at all like proper children,
    which is always very slow.
For he sometimes shoots up taller like
    an India-rubber ball.
And he sometimes gets so little that
    there's none of him at all.

He hasn't got a notion of how children
    ought to play,
And can only make a fool of me
    in every sort of way.
He stays so close beside me,
    he's a coward you can see.
I'd think shame to stick to nursie
    as that shadow sticks to me!

One morning, very early,
    before the sun was up,
I rose and found the shining dew
    on every buttercup.
But my lazy little shadow,
    like an arrant sleepy-head,
Had stayed at home behind me
    and was fast asleep in bed.

A·C·K·N·O·W·L·E·D·G·M·E·N·T·S

Acknowledgment is gratefully made to the following individuals and publishers for permission to reprint these selections.

" 'Who Are You?' Asked the Cat of the Bear." Reprinted with permission of Macmillan Publishing Company from *Away Goes Sally* by Elizabeth Coatsworth. © 1934 by Macmillan Publishing Company, renewed 1962 by Elizabeth Coatsworth Beston.

"The Duck." From *Verses From 1929 On* by Ogden Nash. © 1936 by Ogden Nash. First appeared in the *Saturday Evening Post*. Reprinted by permission of Little, Brown and Company.

"Last Word of a Bluebird (As Told to a Child)." © 1916 by Holt, Reinhart and Winston and renewed 1944 by Robert Frost. Reprinted from *The Poetry of Robert Frost*, edited by Edward Connery Lathem, by permission of Henry Holt and Company, Inc.

"Swahili A B C." Adapted from *Jambo Means Hello* by Muriel Feelings, pictures by Tom Feelings. Text © 1974 by Muriel Feelings. Pictures © 1974 by Tom Feelings. Reprinted by permission of the publisher, Dial Books for Young Readers.

"In Time of Silver Rain." © 1938 and renewed 1966 by Langston Hughes. Reprinted from *Selected Poems of Langston Hughes* by permission of Alfred A. Knopf, Inc.

"André." From *Bronzeville Boys and Girls* by Gwendolyn Brooks. Reprinted by permission of Gwendolyn Brooks.

"My First Word." From *The Story of My Life* by Helen Keller, published by Doubleday, a division of Bantam, Doubleday, Dell Publishing Group, Inc.

"The White Horse." From *The Complete Poems of D. H. Lawrence*, ed. Vivian de Sola Pinto and F. Warren Roberts. © 1964, 1971 by Angelo Ravagli and C. M. Weekley, executors of the estate of Frieda Lawrence Ravagli. All rights reserved. Reprinted by permission of Viking Penguin, a division of Penguin Books USA, Inc.

"The Brocaded Slipper." From *The Brocaded Slipper and Other Vietnamese Tales* by Lynette Dyer Vuong. Text © 1982 by Lynette Dyer Vuong. Reprinted by permission of Harper & Row, Publishers, Inc.

251

The following poems are excerpted from longer poems in consideration of the ages of the readers: "Last Word of a Bluebird" by Robert Frost, "A Bird Came down the Walk" by Emily Dickinson, "In Time of Silver Rain" by Langston Hughes, "The Gingham Dog and the Calico Cat" by Eugene Field, "It Couldn't Be Done" by Edgar A. Guest, and "A Swing Song" by William Allingham.

While the selection appears as originally written, selected words have been replaced to accommodate reading level; obscure references have been clarified; and longer selections have been slightly abbreviated. The following selections have adjusted vocabulary: "The Cat That Walked by Himself" by Rudyard Kipling, "Doctor Dolittle Learns Animal Language" by Hugh Lofting, "The Chimp Who Learned Language" by Anna Michel, "How the Puppet's Nose Grows" by Carlo Collodi, "The Dragon and the Red Cross Knight" by Edmund Spenser, and "Flying with Peter Pan" by J. M. Barrie.

I·L·L·U·S·T·R·A·T·I·O·N C·R·E·D·I·T·S

Acknowledgment is gratefully made to the following for permission to reprint these illustrations.

PAGE	ILLUSTRATOR
11, 13, 15	Pamela R. Levy. © 1991 by Jamestown Publishers, Inc. All rights reserved.
17, 19	Arthur Rackham.
21	Arthur Rackham. The Central Children's Room, Donnell Library Center, The New York Public Library.
22–23	Sir John Tenniel.
25, 37	Rudyard Kipling.
26–27	Thomas Ewing Malloy. © 1991 by Jamestown Publishers, Inc. All rights reserved.
29, 31, 33	Pamela R. Levy. © 1987 by Jamestown Publishers, Inc. All rights reserved.
38–39	Helen Sewell. Reprinted by permission of Macmillan Publishing Company from *Away Goes Sally* by Elizabeth Coatsworth, pictures by Helen Sewell. © 1934 by Macmillan Publishing Company, renewed 1962 by Elizabeth Coatsworth Beston.
41, 43, 46, 48–49, 51 54, 59–60	Unknown.
57	Arthur Rackham. Arthur Rackham Collection, Rare Book and Manuscript Library, Columbia University.
61	N. C. Wyeth. "Mallards in Autumn," h: 9′ 5⅞″ w: 13′ 2¾″. Photographed by Malcolm Varon. Courtesy of Metropolitan Life Insurance Company.

253

62	Alexander Koester. © Courtesy of Art Licensing International, Inc.
63	Alfred Augustus Glendening. © Courtesy of Art Licensing International, Inc.
65	Jan Naimo Jones. © 1991 by Jamestown Publishers, Inc. All rights reserved.
66	Thomas Ewing Malloy. © 1991 by Jamestown Publishers, Inc. All rights reserved.
68–76	Kate Greenaway. Reprinted by permission of The Huntington Library, San Marino, California.
77–88	Wanda Gág. Illustrations by Wanda Gág reprinted by permission of Coward-McCann from *Tales From Grimm* translated and illustrated by Wanda Gág, © 1936 by Wanda Gág, © renewed 1964 by Robert Janssen.
89	Arnold Lobel. From *The Random House Book of Poetry for Children,* selected and introduced by Jack Prelutsky, illustrated by Arnold Lobel. © 1983 by Random House, Inc. Reprinted by permission of the publisher.
92	Thomas Ewing Malloy. © 1991 by Jamestown Publishers, Inc. All rights reserved.
93–95	Tom Feelings. From *Jambo Means Hello* by Muriel Feelings, pictures by Tom Feelings. Pictures © 1974 by Tom Feelings. Reprinted by permission of the publisher, Dial Books for Young Readers.
96	Jessie Willcox Smith. Reprinted by permission of P. S. P. Licensing Corporation.
97, 99, 105, 107	Jessie Willcox Smith.
109	Tom Feelings. © by Tom Feelings.
111–112	Jerry Pinkney. © 1991 by Jamestown Publishers, Inc. All rights reserved.
113, 115	Randolph Caldecott.

117	Courtesy of The Bettmann Archive.
119, 121	Courtesy of American Foundation for the Blind, New York.
123, 125, 127, 129–130	Bob Eggleton. © 1991 by Jamestown Publishers, Inc. All rights reserved.
131	Tom Feelings. © by Tom Feelings.
132	Pamela R. Levy. © 1991 by Jamestown Publishers, Inc. All rights reserved.
135, 139–140	Arthur Rackham. The Central Children's Room, Donnell Library Center, The New York Public Library.
142–144	Arnold Lobel. From *The Random House Book of Poetry for Children,* selected and introduced by Jack Prelutsky, illustrated by Arnold Lobel. © 1983 by Random House, Inc. Reprinted by permission of the publisher.
145–159	Ann G. Barrow. © 1991 by Jamestown Publishers, Inc. All rights reserved.
162–185	Ernest H. Shepard. From *Winnie-the-Pooh* by A. A. Milne, illustrated by Ernest H. Shepard. © 1926 by E. P. Dutton, renewed 1954 by A. A. Milne. Reprinted by permission of the publishers, E. P. Dutton, a division of NAL Penguin, Inc.
188–195	Thomas Ewing Malloy after Hugh Lofting. © 1991 by Jamestown Publishers, Inc. All rights reserved.
197, 199, 201	Herbert S. Terrace. Reprinted by permission of Herbert S. Terrace.
203	Tom Feelings. © by Tom Feelings.
205, 207	Attilio Mussino. Reprinted by permission of Macmillan Publishing Company from *The Adventures of Pinocchio* by Carlo Collodi, illustrated by Attilio Mussino. © 1969 by Macmillan Publishing Company. Illustrations © by Giunti Marzocco, S. P. A., Firenze.
209	Russell Myers. Reprinted by permission of Tribune Media Services.
210	Gelett Burgess.

211	Basil T. Blackwood.
213	Jacob Lawrence.
214	Unknown.
215	Arthur Rackham.
218–219	N. C. Wyeth. Photographs courtesy of the Delaware Art Museum, Wilmington. Reprinted by permission of Houghton Mifflin.
217, 220	Pamela R. Levy. © 1991 by Jamestown Publishers, Inc. All rights reserved.
221	Thomas Ewing Malloy. © 1991 by Jamestown Publishers, Inc. All rights reserved.
223	Arthur Rackham. Rare Book Department, Free Library of Philadelphia.
225, 231, 233	Pamela R. Levy. © 1991 by Jamestown Publishers, Inc. All rights reserved.
227	Arthur Rackham. The Central Children's Room, Donnell Library Center, The New York Public Library.
229	Walter Crane.
235	Robert Gemmel Hutchison. © Courtesy of Art Licensing International, Inc.
237–239, 241–242	Pamela R. Levy. © 1991 by Jamestown Publishers, Inc. All rights reserved.
247	Trina Schart Hyman. Reprinted by permission of Charles Scribner's Sons, an imprint of Macmillan Publishing Company, from the illustrations by Trina Schart Hyman in *Peter Pan* by J. M. Barrie. Illustrations © 1980 by Trina Schart Hyman.
249–250	Jessie Willcox Smith.